The Story of Bermuda and her People

W.S. ZUILL

THIRD EDITION

CARIBBEAN

Dedicated to my wife, Joyce, and our children, Rebecca, Catherine and William

Macmillan Education
Between Towns Road, Oxford OX4 3PP
A division of Macmillan Publishers Limited
Companies and representatives throughout the world

www.macmillan-Caribbean.com

ISBN 0 333 73778 4

First published 1973
Second edition 1983
Third edition 1999

2006 2005 2004 2003
11 10 9 8 7 6

Printed in Malaysia

CONTENTS

Premier

13th October 1997

The Story of Bermuda and Her People is a fascinating chronicle of how the people of Bermuda, with their usual grit and determination, have turned this mid-Atlantic Island into one of the most sophisticated and successful small countries to be found anywhere in the world.

That success has resulted from the blending of resources, of cultures, of experiences, of races and that is something about which every Bermudian can be proud.

Mr. Zuill's latest literary effort encompasses, in broad detail and in fascinating vignettes, the progress of Bermuda's peoples from pre-settlement times through to the monumental periods which saw the end of slavery in Bermuda right up to present-day Bermuda. Along the way, the heroes and heroines who helped shape the destiny of Bermuda are singled out for recognition and come alive for us through the sparkling prose of the author.

This new book, The Story of Bermuda and Her People, is certain to be a rich and valuable resource for students, for amateur historians and for those who are simply interested in the evolution of Bermuda from a rural society into one of the most sophisticated communities anywhere. This is a book that should instill a greater sense of pride in every Bermudian and I have read the manuscript with a sense of interest and fascination and with a greater sense of appreciation of the people and the events that have shaped this beautiful land of ours.

The community owes Mr. Zuill a tremendous debt of gratitude for his scholarship and for this latest contribution to the store of information available about Bermuda and her people.

The Cabinet Office
105 Front Street
Hamilton HM 12
Bermuda
Telephone: 441-292-5501
Fax: 441-292-0304

The Hon. Pamela Gordon, J.P., M.P.

V

INTRODUCTION

This is the history of a small people living on one of the most isolated islands in the globe. It tells how we Bermudians met and are meeting the challenges of the world, striking out to provide a living even though our home contains no mineral resources and only a few small agricultural fields.

Many who live in Bermuda perceive a community split on the basis of skin pigmentation, colour bars and slavery, but a larger view is that despite the problems brought about by this perception we 60 000 inhabitants really have only one culture, formed by a shared history and life on a submarine mountaintop of only 21 and a half square miles, surrounded by an ocean whose varying temperament will produce balmy weather one day and, though rarely, hurricane force winds another.

Thanks to Bermuda's strategic position 564 miles southeast of Cape Hatteras, North Carolina and nearly 800 miles north of the Bahamas, Bermudians have always been in contact with the world around us, and today we islanders form a sophisticated community which has been able to adapt to the need to provide white collar workers for advanced international companies and the banks, accountants and legal firms which support them. The ability to switch skills from hotel work and various artisan trades, as so many have done over the past 45 years, is a hallmark of Bermuda's culture. Another hallmark was shown in the recent debate over whether the Bermuda Government should seek independence from Britain, a debate which was conducted with a lack of emotion and revolved mainly about pragmatic questions of cost and practicability.

This new edition of *The Story of Bermuda and Her People* is a more adult book than the previous editions. It is also more comprehensive. Interest in Bermuda history has taken a great leap forward in the past 25 years, and much new information has been uncovered on such diverse matters as the date of the discovery of Bermuda and the treatment of slaves.

The biggest change since the last edition is the electoral triumph of the Progressive Labour Party on 9 November 1998, breaking the United Bermuda Party's long hold on power, and making the Hon. Miss Jennifer Smith, MP, the Premier. She became leader of the PLP in place of the late Mr Frederick Wade, successor to long-serving Mrs Lois Browne-Evans, MP. Mr Wade had helped to revitalise the PLP before his tragic death. Several other persons have also risen to prominence in the last few years. Ms Pamela Gordon, MP, the outgoing UBP Premier, succeeded Dr David Saul who in turn became Premier on the resignation of Sir John Swan. Sir John was Bermuda's longest-serving Premier, who showed a unique blend of idealism, common sense and understanding of his fellow islanders, but whose dream of leading the island to independence was shattered by a referendum. In trade union affairs Mr Ottiwell Simmons, MP, decided not to seek re-election as President of the leading trade union and was succeeded by Mr Derrick Burgess, MP.

I hope that this book will provide Bermudians with a look at themselves and their ancestors, and give visitors a better idea of our home country. Our motto is *Quo fata ferunt*, which means 'Whither the fates lead us' highly appropriate for an island people who live in the middle of a great ocean and must meet not only the challenges of its many moods but also the varying policies and changing cultures of powerful North Atlantic nations.

W.S. Zuill
Orange Grove
Smith's Parish
Bermuda

ACKNOWLEDGEMENTS

I owe a large debt of gratitude to the outgoing Premier for writing a foreword to this work. She follows in the footsteps of the late Sir Edward Richards, MP, Bermuda's first Premier under a 1973 change in the constitution, who wrote the foreword to earlier editions.

I was encouraged to write this book in the first place by the late Dr Kenneth Robinson, Senior Education Officer, himself an important Bermuda historian and writer. He suggested my name to Mr G.W. Lennox of Macmillan Education as a person who might write a Bermuda history book, and was thereafter of the greatest help. Mr Lennox put his faith in my ability to produce the work, for which I am profoundly grateful. Today Mr Lennox is enjoying a retirement well earned, after spending so many years promoting books for and about Bermuda, the Bahamas and the Caribbean, and his work is carried on by Mr Michael Bourne and Mr Nicolas Gillard.

This book relies in part on several unpublished works: Dr Robinson's thesis on the history of education in Bermuda; Mr Ottiwell Simmons' thesis on the history of industrial trade unionism in Bermuda; Mrs Dee Block's history of the first 25 years of the Bermuda base at the airfield, and Mrs Sandy Tatem's history of the US Navy in Bermuda.

No work on Bermuda history would be complete without acknowledging the great debt Bermuda owes the late Dr Henry Wilkinson, whose four volumes covering the history of Bermuda from the 17th to the 19th Century are of the utmost value to the serious researcher and reader. They are his enduring monument, and will give him an honoured place long after the community leaders of our time have passed from the memory of our grandchildren.

I would also like to acknowledge the general debt all island historians owe Major General Sir J. H. Lefroy, one-time Governor, whose *Memorials of the Bermudas* put the major part of the early documents relating to Bermuda's early history in print.

Among those who have helped me either through their published works or personally are Dr Edward Harris, Miss Eva Hodgson, Mrs Barbara Harries Hunter, Mrs Albert Jackson, Sister Jean de Chantal Kennedy, Mr Wayne Little, Mr Ira Philip, Dr E.S.D. Ratteray, Mr George Rushe, Mr James Smith, Dr Wolfgang Sterrer, Mr Robert Stewart, Mrs Terry Tucker, Dr David Wingate, the staffs of Ministries of Tourism and of Technology and Information, the Statistics Department and the office of the Registrar General. In particular I would like to thank the Bermuda Library staff, especially the late Mr Cyril Outerbridge Packwood and his successor Ms Grace Rawlings, and the staff of the Bermuda Archives and the several Archivists who have cared for this treasure house of Bermuda historical material. The responsibility for any errors is mine.

Finally I want to thank my mother and father for originating my interest in history and for much information, both verbal and through the pages of their writing. I owe a particular debt to my brother Mr James V. Zuill, for his constant encouragement.

But above all I wish to thank my wife for her support, understanding, patience and help both in the original writing of this book and then, all over again, in the rewriting of this present edition.

W.S. Zuill

Photographic acknowledgements

The author and publisher wish to acknowledge the sources of the following photographs:

Bermuda News Bureau, pp. 6, 7, 12, 17, 19, 21, 35, 37, 39, 49, 54, 56, 61, 66, 75, 77, 87, 92, 102, 104, 121, 133, 140, 146, 150, 152, 160, 168, 169, 191, 201, 206, 208, 239, 241, 246; Bermuda National Trust, pp. 175; Bermuda Historical Society, p. 21; Mansell Collection, p. xiv; Radio Times Hulton Picture Library, pp. 84, 106; Dave Saunders, pp. 34, 238; Scottcraft, p. 207.
Cover photograph: Dave Saunders
Other photographs courtesy of the author

LIST OF ILLUSTRATIONS

Photographs/etchings

Maps

PROLOGUE

Week after week the three small ships had sailed across the Atlantic, constantly heading westward, pushed by the prevailing winds. It had not been a stormy voyage, but when would it end?

It took incredible courage to keep going into the unknown, into seas which no one knew. At one stage the men's courage failed and there was an attempt to make the Admiral turn back. He refused, but soon he knew he would have to reverse his course, for supplies were running low.

Then signs of land began to appear, branches and land birds. At last, on 12 October 1492 the glad news rang out: 'Land!'

It was an island and the Admiral, Christopher Columbus, named it San Salvador. It was an outrider of many other islands and of the great continent of America, stretching from the Arctic Circle almost to the Antarctic. We now know that others had sailed across the Atlantic before Columbus, but their achievements were forgotten.

Before 1492 the Atlantic was a great barrier; since then it has become a highway between the continents. That is why the story of Columbus is important to us in Bermuda, as it is to every part of the Americas.

The way now was open and Bermuda was discovered not long after the Admiral set foot on San Salvador. Columbus himself might well have discovered the archipelago on his homeward voyage. He sailed north from the Caribbean until he was close to our latitudes before he turned east to head back to Spain and a hero's welcome.

Columbus on board his ship

PART 1

Pre-settlement Bermuda

1

The Curtain Rises

Who discovered Bermuda and when they did is not clear. Ancient legends tell of an Irish monk named St Brendan who explored the Atlantic in the mid-sixth century, and one of the legends could refer to Bermuda. It tells of an island with birds chattering at sunset, an isolated island far from any other land, discovered by St Brendan on a voyage on which he was accompanied by other monks. Whether St Brendan actually existed and did all that he is credited with is an unanswered historical question. It may be that Irish monks did sail across the Atlantic and returned to tell the tale; the ocean has been crossed a number of times in cockleshells, including a replica of a sea-going coracle made of pieces of leather sewed together and stretched across a boat-shaped frame.

No ancient bones of land mammals such as rats appear anywhere. On the other hand the bones of ancient birds are fairly plentiful, indicating that mammals only arrived with the Spanish. If there were visitors in the sixth century they have left no trace. What the truth is we are never likely to know, but sometimes ancient legends are unexpectedly shown to be true and therefore should not be completely dismissed.

The St Brendan story is commemorated in Bermuda by the use of his name for a hospital. In fact, the discovery of Bermuda was made almost certainly by Spaniards. In 1511 a map was published in an atlas called the *Legatio Babylonica* which included Bermuda under the name of La Bermuda. The Spanish historian Herrera says the island was discovered by Juan de Bermudez in command of a ship called *La Garza (The Heron)*, and David B. Quinn, in an article published in the *Bermuda Journal of Archaeology and Maritime History*, thinks it likely that Bermuda was found in 1505 or 1506, for in 1505 Bermudez, a veteran sea captain, sailed in La Garza from Spain bound for Hispaniola. As 1505/6 ties in well with the publication in 1511, it seems likely that the discovery took place in one of these two years.

The placement on a map did not provide a description of the island. An inkling of what it was like was provided in 1515 when Gonzales Ferdinando d'Oviedo sighted Bermuda and tried to land some pigs with the idea that they would become wild, and would be available as food for the crew of any ship which came close to the island or was wrecked. D'Oviedo failed to land the pigs because the wind made it too difficult to sail close to the island, but he wrote a description of Bermuda's size, and added the charming passage (as translated by Richard Eden):

> While I remayned here I saw a strife and combat between these flying fishes and the fishes named giltheads, and the fowles called sea mewes, and cormorants, which surely seemed unto me a thing of as great pleasure and solace as could be devised. While the giltheads swam on the brim of the water, and sometimes lifted their shoulders above the same, to raise the flying fishes out of the water to drive them to flight, and follow them swimming to the place where they fall, to take and eate them suddenly. Again, on the other side, the sea mewes and cormorants, take many of these flying fishes, so that by this means they are neither safe in the Aire, nor in the water. In the self-same perill and danger doe men live in this mortal life, wherein is no certaine securities, neither in high estate, nor in lowe. Which thing surely ought to put us in remembrance of the blessed and safe resting place which God hath prepared for such as love him who shall acquit and finish the travailes of this troublesome world, wherein are so many dangers, and bring them to that Eternall life where they shall find eternal security and rest.

The route Columbus took on his homeward voyage became a favourite track for ships bound from the Caribbean to Spain. All sailing ships can waste a great deal of time working their way against the wind, and this was even more true in Columbus's time. The Spaniards needed a route where they were blown or pushed by favourable winds or currents. By sailing north up the Gulf Stream

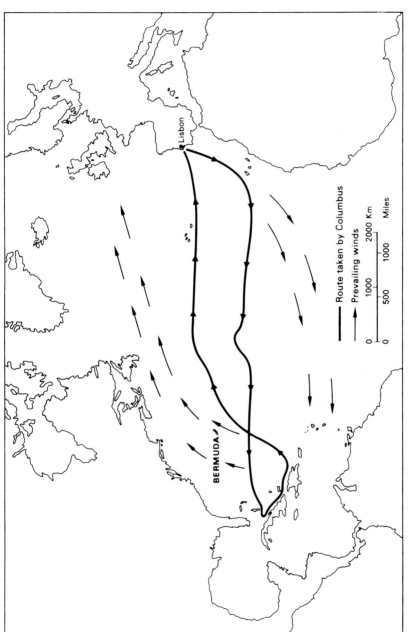

The route taken by Columbus

Lisbon

BERMUDA

Route taken by Columbus
Prevailing winds

0   1000   2000 Km
0   500   1000   Miles

they were able to work themselves clear of the belt of easterly winds until they reached the latitude of Bermuda, where the winds are more likely to be westerly and helpful.

Bermuda stood alone amongst thousands of square miles of ocean. There were no other islands or rocks in these latitudes, and the navigators had to be extremely careful to avoid hitting this island, with its dangerous hidden reefs running out to sea. Not all ships succeeded, for sometimes navigators made mistakes, and sometimes storms drove ships onto Bermuda.

Since the Second World War the use of aqualung equipment has made underwater exploration much easier, and although through the ages many Bermudians have dived to explore and salvage from wrecks, much more has been found in recent times. Two Bermudian divers in particular, Mr Teddy Tucker and the late Mr Harry Cox, have made important discoveries in our reef-ridden waters. One of Mr Cox's finds was an astrolabe, which in the time we are talking about was one of the few instruments navigators had for obtaining the height of the sun or stars and thus their latitude. His discovery is one of the few extant astrolabes left in the world.

The late Mr Harry Cox with a Spanish astrolabe

Mr Teddy Tucker with treasure from a Spanish wreck,
now on display in the Aquarium Museum

Today there is concern about the indiscriminate removal of artifacts from wreck sites without thought as to what they mean in uncovering more information about the past, and many countries, including Bermuda, have laws to try and stop outright plundering of heritage shipwrecks. Archaeological diving has taken place on more than one wreck, and the salvage by the Maritime Museum of the remaining timbers of what is believed to be a Spanish despatch ship and the work of the Sea Venture Trust show what can be done.

The Portuguese and Bermuda

The Spanish made no attempt to settle Bermuda, but in 1527 the Portuguese nearly did so. A man from the Azores named Ferdinand Camelo received permission to bring colonists to Bermuda, but as far as is known nothing came of it. The first Portuguese on the island appears to have arrived in 1543, some 16 years later, and left behind a carving on a rock at Spittal Pond, Smith's Parish, a replica of which is there now. Thanks to information sent to the Bermuda Historical Quarterly by Senor J. Vidago of Caracas, Venezuela, it is now known that in that year a Portuguese ship bound for Portugal from the city of Santo Domingo, in what is now the Dominican Republic, was wrecked on an unknown and isolated island which seems likely to have been Bermuda, for several details in the story, which is given by Oviedo, fit Bermuda. The vessel was wrecked on the north reefs, and was thought to be four leagues from land (12 miles). All thirty of the crew came safely ashore and built a ship in which they returned to Santo Domingo.

Many years later the rock carving was discovered and was called Spanish Marks. The date was clear – 1543 – but the initials were not. They could have been R and a cross; but Vidago thought it might well be a monogram of RP, which with the cross could form the badge of the Portuguese Order of Christ – *Rex Portugaliae*. There can scarcely be any doubt now that the carving was made by a member of the ship's company, perhaps as he kept watch over the ocean hoping to see a vessel coming from the West Indies which would take him and his friends from the deserted island.

The carving itself no longer exists. A well-meaning attempt to save it by enclosing it in a wooden box with a glass top resulted in its crumbling away, apparently because the sun on the glass caused intense heat to concentrate on the rock. Fortunately a plaster of Paris casting had been made (it or a similar casting is owned by the Bermuda Historical Society Museum in Hamilton) and from it a brass casting was made and placed where the old inscription had crumbled.

Early French and English Visitors

The first French people known to have come to Bermuda also arrived because they were shipwrecked. This happened sometime between 1560 and 1570. Again a boat was made, and on this occasion the men sailed north to Newfoundland, where they probably met a vessel from the great cod fishing fleet which has congregated off the Grand Banks since 1500 or thereabouts, or perhaps even earlier.

The first known Englishman to visit here arrived on board a French ship in 1593. It was a dark night in December, but the ship's navigator had assured the captain that there was no danger of running into Bermuda. For this he was rewarded with liquor, known as his 'wine of height', for navigating the ship safely that far – and perhaps this had a bearing on what happened next, for as the ship drove on it suddenly struck a reef (perhaps North Rock) which towered out of the water.

The crew built a raft, but even so there was room for only half of them on the raft and in the ship's boat. The Englishman, Henry May, hesitated to get in the boat, but Captain de la Barbotiere told him to get aboard and after many hours of rowing they came safely to shore. It seems likely that the rest of crew were saved later. A vessel was built which took them all to Newfoundland and the Grand Banks, where they found a passage home.

The Story of Venturilla

The first known black man to come to Bermuda was called Venturilla and he arrived on board a Spanish ship commanded by Captain Diego Ramirez. Ramirez was skipper of one of five treasure galleons homeward bound for Spain. Early in the voyage they ran into a storm, and Captain Ramirez's ship struck the rocks of Bermuda. Luckily for them all, the ship was forced across the reefs and into Great Sound.

When Ramirez's ship anchored in the bay night was falling and the captain sent a small boat ashore to find water. Darkness crept over the land and, as happens today, birds started chattering; but there were many more birds then.

One bird song, probably that of the shearwater, sounded to the Spaniards like 'Diselo, diselo', which means 'Tell them' in English. A seaman on the ship said: 'What is this devil trying to tell me? Out with it! Let us hear what it is!' Captain Ramirez, remembering all the seamen's tales about devils living on Bermuda, and about the island being enchanted, said: 'Ah, these are the devils of Bermuda, which they say are hereabouts. The sign of the cross at them! We are Christians!'

The captain's words probably frightened the seamen a little more, and just at that moment the small boat shot alongside. The men clambered up the side of the ship exclaiming: 'What devils are these? The boat's rudder is broken.'

Captain Ramirez by now was in better control of himself, and ordered another rudder to be made immediately, because the boat would have to be used in the morning to search for water, and without a rudder it would be difficult to handle. He ordered Venturilla to go ashore and cut a piece of wood for a new rudder. Despite his fears, Venturilla obeyed. Perhaps, as his name suggests, he was eager for adventure. He landed with his lantern and disappeared in the bushes. Then he began to yell.

Ramirez shouted: 'The devil is carrying off the Negro. All ashore!'

Men tumbled into the boat and rapidly rowed ashore, where they too began to yell as unseen enemies rushed at them out of the dark. As they hit and clubbed, one or two of the men with cooler heads discovered the attackers were not devils, but birds, and were probably good to eat, too. So they killed 500 of them, brought them to the ship, cooked them and enjoyed them very much; indeed they lived off them most of the rest of their stay in Bermuda.

Captain Ramirez drew a map of the island and also set up a large cross with directions on it in Spanish telling future visitors where to find drinking water. This was later taken as an indication of buried treasure, and a map drawn by English settlers from the cross has been mistaken as a treasure map up to the present day. Remains of a camp have also been found, and ever since the area has been known as Spanish Point.

The next known shipwreck was a momentous one for Bermuda, because it led to the settlement of these islands by Englishmen nearly 400 years ago. This story is told in the next chapter.

SOURCES
Lefroy, *Memorials of the Bermudas* (third edition).
Bermuda Historical Quarterly Vol. 7, No. 2 (April, May, June 1950), and
    Vol. 19, No. 2.
Bermuda Journal of Archaeology and Maritime History, Vol. 1 (1989).
    Wilkinson, *The Adventurers of Bermuda* (2nd edition).

2

The Great Storm

In the year 1610 William Strachey sat down at a crude table in a hut in Jamestown, Virginia, to write the story of a notable shipwreck, how a ship's company had been saved, and how they had fared on an uninhabited island. Dipping his quill pen into the ink, he began with the sailing of a fleet from England the year before.

Seven ships and two smaller vessels, called pinnaces, gathered at Plymouth to carry supplies and colonists to the tiny, weak English settlement up the James River from Chesapeake Bay, a settlement which had been started just two years before. This was the nucleus from which the great English-speaking United States was to grow, but it was so small and poor a nucleus that time and time again it was barely saved. Indeed, it was the first English settlement to survive. Other attempts at colonization had been made, but they had failed.

The largest ship in the fleet was the *Sea Venture*, 300 tons, broad in the beam, built to carry goods and people safely over the dangerous sea. She was the flagship, and aboard her were the Admiral of the Fleet, Sir George Somers; the Governor-designate of Jamestown, Sir Thomas Gates;[1] the Captain of the ship, Christopher Newport (who had headed the first expedition to Jamestown); and Strachey, who hoped for an appointment as Virginia's Secretary.

There were lots of other people aboard too. There were gentlemen – one in particular named Henry Paine. There was a wealthy lady, Mistress Horton, and her maid. There was a priest, the Rev. Richard Bucke. There was a man who one day was to discover how to cure Virginia tobacco so that it was pleasant for English tastes,

Sir Thomas Gates

and who also was to marry the Indian Princess Pocahontas. He was John Rolfe, and he was travelling with his first wife, who was pregnant. There was also Sylvester Jourdan, whose own report gives some details Strachey omits.

Also aboard were two men who were not going to Virginia to settle but were going home. They were American Indians named Matchumps and Namuntuck, and they had been persuaded to go to England by Captain John Smith, that amazing and extraordinary adventurer who at this time was holding Virginia together.

There were also working people and sailors, probably all white, but there may have been black people among them for a number of black people resided in England in 1609. Plymouth, at the mouth of the English Channel, was a good place to start for the Americas, and on 2 June 1609 the fleet set sail under Sir George Somers' orders. Sir George was an experienced mariner who had made a small fortune during the long war with Spain which ended in 1603, and who had been second-in-command of an expedition to what is now Venezuela under Sir Amyas Preston. Now he, like Sir Thomas Gates, was a shareholder in the Virginia Company with headquarters in London (there was another Virginia Company with headquarters in Plymouth).

Sir George felt that previous voyages had wasted much time in sailing as far south as the Canary Islands and crossing the Atlantic to the West Indies before turning north to Jamestown, and he directed the fleet on a course which traversed the middle of the North Atlantic. Taking this new course was a big change.

The voyage went well. The fleet stayed together, and day after day the vessels made progress. Each day the sun came up, revealing nothing but sea all around, the sails bellied, the wind whistled through the rigging, the water bubbled and hissed as it slid along the hulls, and the wooden ribs and planking creaked as the ships rose and fell in the Atlantic waves. The only incident was that one of the smaller vessels, a pinnace, turned back to England. The other pinnace was towed by the *Sea Venture* so that her slow speed would not delay the fleet.

Then on a day when Captain Newport estimated that they were about a week away from Chesapeake Bay, the weather changed, and as the evening grew to darkness heavy clouds covered the sky, hiding the stars. When dawn came the waves had become steeper and more menacing and the wind was singing a new and more sinister note in the rigging. The weather made it dangerous for the *Sea Venture* to continue towing the pinnace and the small vessel was cast adrift, never to be seen again. The captains and crews of the ships soon had their hands full coping with the storm, and quickly the vessels disappeared from one another's sight. Only the *Sea Venture* and the pinnace failed to reach Jamestown; the rest arrived there safely.

Aboard the *Sea Venture* the sails were now furled; an attempt to show even a small corner of canvas meant that it took six to eight men to handle the tiller and whipstaff, which was the equivalent of a

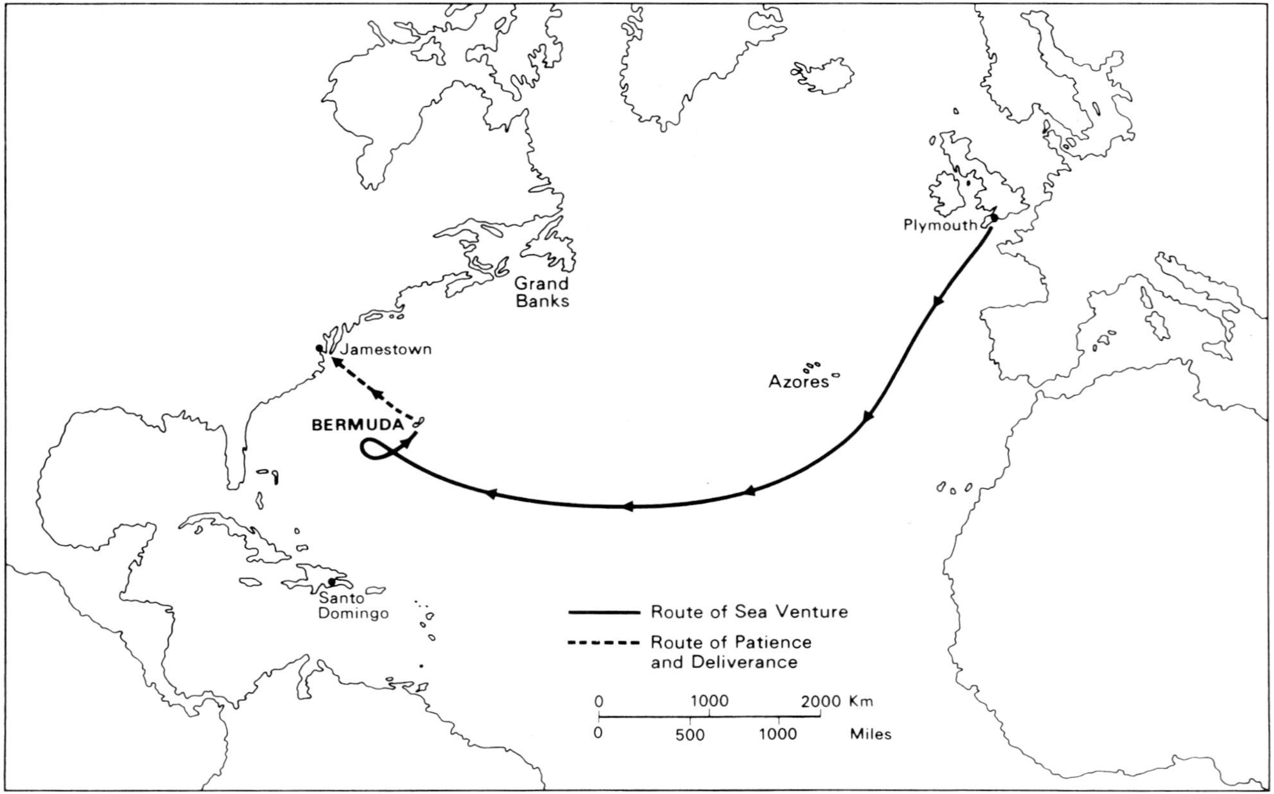

The route of Sea Venture

Plymouth

Azores

Grand
Banks

Jamestown

BERMUDA

Santo
Domingo

Route of Sea Venture
Route of Patience
and Deliverance

Miles
2000 Km
1000
1000
500
0
0

14

steering wheel in those days. The *Sea Venture* was in a difficult situation, but soon there was more to fear when a sailor discovered that the ship was leaking, and leaking badly.

The pumps were manned immediately, and the crew searched the vessel for leaks. They found a great number and stuffed them up as well as they could, using cloth and even beef, but still the water poured in. What had happened was that the fierce waves of the hurricane had battered the planking, pulling and pressing it so that the movement had released the caulking from between the planks and there was nothing to stop the water from coming in.

It was a desperate situation. The ship was alone, rolling and pitching, helpless in the enormous waves. The sea was pouring in, '... to me,' Strachey wrote at his table in Jamestown, 'this leak appeared as a wound, given to men that were before [i.e. already] dead.'

He remembered wondering whether it was worth fighting on. 'Yet we did,' he said, 'either because so dear are a few lingering hours of life in all mankind, or that our Christian knowledge taught us how much we owed ... not to be false to ourselves or to neglect the means of our own preservation ...'

At this point Sir Thomas Gates showed why he had been chosen to be a Governor. He divided the crew and passengers into three groups, and each group worked away at the pumps and at bailing for an hour, and then rested. The bailing was hard; small barrels had to be filled with water below decks and hoisted from one person to another up to the main deck to be poured out. Both Sir Thomas and Sir George Somers took part in the work, although Sir George was also busy overseeing the steering and attempting to ease the ship's way through the harsh and cruel sea.

One enormous wave broke over the stern; water filled the deck of the centre section so that only the forecastle and the poop were above the sea. The shock knocked men off their feet and made Strachey think the *Sea Venture* was gone; but slowly the ship rose up and continued her mad career northward, a plaything of both wind and wave.

The storm had hit on Tuesday 25 June, and the leak started the same day. By Thursday everyone's spirits were flagging as they continued their desperate day and night battle against the in-pouring sea. That night St Elmo's fire appeared in the rigging. Strachey called it 'an apparition of a little round light, like a faint star, trembling and streaming along with a sparkling blaze, half the height upon the mainmast, and shooting sometimes from shroud to shroud ... and for three or four hours together ... it kept with us, running sometimes along the mainyard to the very end and then returning.'

It was frightening to some of the crew, but Strachey and a number of others knew that this phenomenon occurred sometimes in storms. We now know that it is an electrical discharge, a sort of mini-lightning, a function of static electricity.

When dawn came on Friday the storm seemed just as bad, and the ship's company were giving up the struggle. In a desperate attempt to keep the ship afloat they started to lighten her, throwing trunks and stores overboard, and even the ship's starboard cannon. The morning wore on, and all around was a waste of water. More people gave up hope, stopped bailing, pulled out bottles of brandy – according to Sylvester Jourdan they gave toasts to 'their more joyful meeting in a more blessed world.' Did they prefer to drown drunk rather than sober?

Sir George was on the high poop, and while everyone's attention was concentrated in the ship he looked up and out – and sighted land. It was Bermuda.[2]

The island was quite close, for they could see trees waving in the fierce wind, and the sight gave the passengers and crew new courage. They started bailing the *Sea Venture* again. Sails were set and the ship drove eastward down the South Shore, slowly working in closer to land. Finally they reached St David's Head and rounded to, protected from the wind and sea, but the *Sea Venture* still leaked as badly as ever. Then Sir George ordered the ship to be headed for shore, and after travelling another mile the vessel bumped over a reef and stuck fast between two rocks. Her remains are in the vicinity to this day.

Sir Thomas Gates jumped into the first boat, as was his right as land commander, and went ashore. As he reached land (at St Catherine's Beach) he shouted 'Gates, his bay!' During the afternoon the *Sea Venture*'s boat plied back and forth, and by nightfall everyone was ashore. They were safe, but now they faced dangers from each other.

This reconstruction shows survivors of the Sea Venture
wreck struggling ashore at St Catherine's Beach

NOTES
1. A portrait of Sir Thomas Gates is in the care of the Bermuda National Trust, and for some years has been hung upstairs over the stairway in the Cabinet Building.
2. There have been many theories about the course of the *Sea Venture* in the storm and what part of Bermuda Sir George Somers sighted. The theory used here is that of Mr Cyril Smith, who also made plans and a model of the *Deliverance* from which the full-scale replica in St George's was made.

SOURCES
Hakluyt, *The Principal Navigations, Voyages, Traffiques & Discoveries of the English Nation.*
Lefroy, *Memorials of the Bermudas* (3rd edition).
Smith, *The Generall Historie of Virginia.*

3

Mutinies and Murders

From the start Sir George and Sir Thomas did not get along. Sir George, who was known as 'a lamb on shore but a lion at sea', had been in supreme command on the *Sea Venture*, but on shore Sir Thomas, as the future Governor of Virginia, was in charge. Sea commanders and land commanders have often disagreed and in their disagreement caused a great deal of trouble, and this was one of the reasons why the *Sea Venture* people did not have a happy time on the island.

The ship's company stayed in Bermuda for nine months before they completed the construction of two small ships and sailed safely to Virginia. One of these was the *Deliverance*. Exactly what she looked like we do not know, but Strachey gives her size and from what he said and from a knowledge of ships of the time a full-scale replica was constructed by the Junior Service League at St George's. The replica gives a good idea not only of the *Deliverance* but of ships in the 17th century in general. Passengers were crammed in the narrow between-decks with cargo below them and the main deck above, the hatch opening often guarded by a grating or completely covered over in bad weather. Cooking could only be carried out over an open fire in comparatively calm weather: wooden ships were always in danger from fire at sea. The toilets for most people were over the sea at the 'heads' at the bow beside the bowsprit, but slops were often thrown down into the bilges.

The original *Deliverance* was built under the direction of the *Sea Venture*'s carpenter, Richard Frobisher, and the bay at which he built her was named Frobisher's Buildings Bay. Today it is called Buildings

Sir George Somers

Bay, and seems to have been chosen without much foresight. During gales the vessel was in danger of being washed away by heavy seas, and was barely saved. Her ribs and much of the rest of the vessel were made of materials taken from the *Sea Venture* wreck. The other vessel was the *Patience*. She was built under the supervision of Sir George elsewhere away from the main camp, and was entirely of Bermuda cedar with only one iron bolt from the *Sea Venture*.

When the *Sea Venture* company came ashore Sir Thomas was acutely concerned to get word to Virginia. His responsibilities lay there, and he was anxious to move on and take up his duties. He knew that he would be superseded when Lord de la Warr came to Jamestown. And so the *Sea Venture*'s longboat was fitted with a deck, eight men boarded her and with Master's Mate Henry Ravens in command she set sail for Virginia.

Work on the *Deliverance* started before Ravens sailed – after all, if the other vessels had perished in the storm there might be no rescue ship at Jamestown – but there was every reason to hope that his mission would be successful. Ravens thought he would be back in a month's time, and in September Strachey was put in charge of a bonfire built on St David's Head and set to keep watch for the longboat. He spent two months watching, but Ravens and his men never turned up. In fact they disappeared at sea.

Probably unhappy at being cooped up in a camp under Gates, Sir George built a cedar boat and set out on a voyage of exploration of Bermuda. As he went he made a map, one copy of which is in the Bermuda Archives. It is remarkably accurate, far more so than the one made by Ramirez, which is obviously a rough sketch of the Great Sound. Sir George's map contains four pictures, two of them fanciful and two of them showing men getting food by fishing and by hunting. The hunters are accompanied by the ship's dog and are hunting pigs, or 'hogs', which they found in great abundance, thanks either to some Spanish captain like d'Oviedo or to a shipwreck. At the time the *Sea Venture* was wrecked the pigs were fat from eating cedar and palmetto berries; later they lost their fat when the berry season ended. Then the settlers started living on turtles and later cahows (sea birds) and of course, fish. They also used the stores they could salvage from the *Sea Venture*, but these were carefully rationed.

Sir Thomas ran into difficulties as he tried to make the crew and passengers labour on the *Deliverance*. Even though he set an example by working as hard as anyone, many of the passengers and crew objected to the hard work, such as hewing down cedar trees and cutting them into planks with hand saws, trimming wood with adzes, preparing wooden treenails (fasteners), and said: 'Why don't we just stay here, where there is lots of food and not much work to do to get it?'

A man name Nicholas Bennet was the first to start talking in this way, and he soon persuaded a small group that he was right.

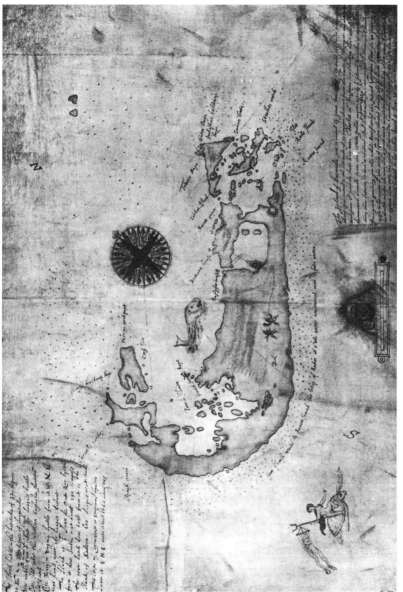

Map of Bermuda made by Sir George Somers

One of his followers was Christopher Carter – who in fact stayed in Bermuda for many years and died here; he was the first settler, and later became Governor for a short time: it seems likely that many Bermudians living today are descended from him. Sir Thomas sent Bennet and his followers to live on a small island by themselves, but pretty soon they found they did not like it, and Sir Thomas allowed them to return.

The second mutiny was a one-man affair. Stephen Hopkins, who had a degree of education, also wanted to stay on the island. Sir Thomas ordered Hopkins to be shot, but, says Strachey, 'So penitent he was, and made so much moan, alleging the ruin of his wife and children in this his trespass, as it wrought in the hearts of the better sort of the company, who therefore with humble entreaties and earnest supplications went unto our Governor ...'. Sir Thomas relented, and Hopkins survived to return to England and go out to America again in 1620 aboard the Mayflower. He and the Pilgrim Fathers disagreed, but he lived out his life in America.

The third mutiny could have been by far the most serious. A group of men planned to kill the Governor, seize the storehouse and make off with whatever tools and food they needed. Most of those involved were helping to build the *Patience* under the command of Sir George. Sir Thomas heard about the plot and ordered every man to carry a weapon with him at all times. He also doubled the night watch. This prevented the conspirators from taking any action but everyone remained uneasy.

Then on the evening of 13 March 1610, Henry Paine, one of the conspirators, was ordered to go on watch. He refused and said the Governor could 'kiss ... .' Next day Paine was tried and sentenced to be hanged immediately. Paine confessed what he had been up to, and asked, since he was a gentleman, to be shot instead of hanged, 'and towards evening,' says Strachey, 'he had his desire, the sun and his life setting together.'

News of Paine's execution reached Sir George's boatbuilding camp and many of the twenty men who were with him immediately ran into the woods for fear that Paine had given their names as being involved in the plot (in fact he refused to implicate anyone else). Not only that, but they also asked Sir George for a store of meal and clothing.

Did Sir George sympathize with them? Strachey does not say so, but reading between the lines it seems likely. The conspirators were probably all sailors, not passengers, and there is reason to think that Sir George had a special feeling for them. Also, it is obvious that Sir George himself had fallen in love with Bermuda and perhaps was not anxious to leave.

By this time Sir George and Sir Thomas were cold and distant with each other, but the danger of mutiny was so serious that Sir Thomas decided to try and heal the breach. He wrote a long letter to Sir George, urging him to seek out the runaway seamen and 'by the virtue of that ancient love and friendship, which has these many years been settled between them', to do his best to make the men return to their duty.

Sir George was moved by the letter, and in the end succeeded in bringing back all the sailors except Christopher Carter and Robert Waters. Waters was a murderer; he had killed another seaman named Edward Samuell with a shovel, and had been sentenced to death, but his fellow sailors had helped him to escape. Carter did not return because he was convinced that, having rebelled twice, he would be punished by Sir Thomas.

There was another murder, a secret one. John Smith tells about it: 'some ... differences fell between them, that Matchumps slew Namuntuck, and having made a hole to bury him, because it was too short, he cut off his legs and laid them by him, which murder he concealed till he was in Virginia.'

During the stay on the island two children were born, a girl named Bermuda and a boy named Bermudas. Bermuda was the daughter of John Rolfe, but she died here soon after she was born.

It seems significant and symbolic of their different natures that Gates, anxious to get on, named his vessel the *Deliverance*, while Somers named his the *Patience*. Still, they pulled together sufficiently so that the two vessels sailed from Bermuda in company on 12 May, leaving Carter and Waters behind.

Rescue at Jamestown

The *Patience* and *Deliverance* took only ten days to reach Chesapeake Bay, and soon afterwards were working their way up the James River to Jamestown. The settlement was in a shocking state. Only 60 people were alive out of the 500 who were there the autumn before, supplies had nearly run out, and the *Sea Venture* survivors from Bermuda, instead of finding help after all their troubles, became the rescuers of the colony.

Although the *Patience* and *Deliverance* brought good supplies of food, there was not enough to keep the whole of Jamestown going, so it was decided to abandon the colony, using the two Bermuda-built pinnaces and two vessels at Jamestown to sail to the Grand Banks in the hope of finding help from the fishing fleet.

On 7 June Jamestown was abandoned and the fleet set sail down the river. On the same day a new supply fleet, with Lord de la Warr aboard, was putting into the mouth of the river. The vessels met, and all put back to Jamestown.

'The Lord's infinite goodnesse'

There were those who saw the series of events which saved Jamestown as the hand of God. Captain Smith's *General History of Virginia*, quoting a report issued in England by the Virginia Company, puts it this way:

> Hee that shall but turne up his eie and behold the spangled canopie of heaven, or shall but cast down his eie, and consider the embroydered carpet of the earth, and withall shall marke how the heavens heare the earth, and the earth the Corne and Oile, and they relieve the necessities of man, that man will acknowledge God's infinite providence: But hee that shall further observe, how God inclineth all casual events to worke the necessary helpe of his Saints, must needs adore the Lords infinite goodnesse; never had any people more just cause, to cast themselves at the very foot-stoole of God, and to reverence his mercie, than this distressed Colonie; for if God had not sent Sir Thomas Gates from the Bermudas, within four daies they had almost beene famished; if God had not directed the heart of that noble Knight to save the Fort from fiering at their shipping, for many were very importunate to have burnt it, they had beene destitute of a present harbour and succour; if they had abandoned the Fort any longer time, and had not so soone returned, questionlesse the Indians would have destroied the Fort, which had beene the means of our safeties amongst them

and a terror. If they had set saile sooner, and had lanched into the vast Ocean, who would have promised they should have encountered the Fleet of the Lord la Warre ... ?

There was still the practical problem of laying in a further supply of food so the colonists would not starve during the coming winter, and Sir George offered to take the *Patience* on a fishing expedition and to return to Bermuda for other supplies. He sailed in company with Captain Samuel Argall, a man who would soon make his mark by attacking French settlements in Maine and Nova Scotia. Somers and Argall sailed north along the coast, but lost touch with each other in fog. Argall returned to Jamestown while Somers continued on to Bermuda.

Death of Sir George Somers

In Bermuda Sir George died. John Smith says:

> ... but such was his diligence with his extraordinary care, paines and industry to dispatch his businesse, and the strength of his body not answering the ever memorable courage of his minde, having lived so long in such honourable services, the most part of his well beloved and vertuous life ...: finding his time but short, after he had taken the best course he could to settle his estate, like a valiant Captaine he exhorted them with all diligence to be constant to those Plantations, and with all expedition to returne to Virginia. In that very place which we now call Saint Georges towne, this noble knight died, whereof the place taketh the name.

Smith's statement indicates that St George's was named, in a 17th century play on words, for both the saint and the admiral. It is a strong argument for dropping the possessive apostrophe and simply making the name of the town and the parish plural – St Georges.

Sir George's nephew Matthew sailed with him to Bermuda and took command of the *Patience* after his uncle's death. He decided to return to England, taking the Admiral's body with him – perhaps to ensure that people would believe that Sir George was indeed dead, for he had been reported dead once when the *Sea Venture* failed to arrive at Jamestown, and once before that had been despaired of when his ship arrived long after her due time. Carter and two other men, Chard and Waters (a different Waters from the murderer of Samuell) were left behind.

When Matthew finally arrived in England he and his crew told many tales about Bermuda, and letters arriving from Virginia confirmed what they said. This aroused tremendous interest, and the Virginia Company decided to send colonists to the island.

Mementoes and Memorial of Sir George

When the opportunity came at Jamestown to send letters back to England Sir George sat down to write his report, which tells a good deal about his personality. He wrote:[1]

> Right honourable:
> May it please your good honour to be advised that our departure out of England in going to Virginia about some 200 leagues from the Bermudas we were taken with a very great storm or hurricane which sundered all the fleet and on St James's Day being the 23rd of July we had such a leak in our ship insomuch that there was nine foot of water before we knew of any such thing. We pumped with two pumps and bailed in three or four places with certain barricoes and then we kept a hundred men always working night and day from the 23rd until the 28th of the same July, being Friday, at which time we saw the island of Bermuda, where our ship lieth upon the rock, a quarter of a mile distant from the shore where we saved all our lives and afterwards saved much of our goods, but all our bread was wet and lost.
>
> We continued in the island from the 28th July until the 10th of May, in which time we built two small barques to carry our people to Virginia the 23rd of the same month and coming to Cape Henry the captain there told us of the famine that was at Jamestown, whereupon we hastened up there and found it true, for they had eaten all the quick things that were there and some of them had eaten snakes or adders.
>
> But by the industry of our Governor in the Bermudas [Sir Thomas Gates] there was saved a little meal ... and [we]

recovered all save three that were past recovering before our coming.

We consulted together what course were best to be taken for our means would not continue above fourteen days.

We thought good to take into our four pinnaces as much of the munition as we could and took in all the people and were going down the river but by the way we met with the Lord Delawar ... which made our hearts very glad, and we presently returned up to Jamestown and there we found no savages for they were afraid to come thither.

Now we are in good hope to plant and abide here for here is a good course taken and a greater care than ever there was.

I am going to the Bermudas for fish and hogs with two small pinnaces and am in good opinion to be back again before the Indians do gather their harvest.

Bermuda is the most plentiful place that ever I came to, for fish, hogs and fowl.

Thus wishing all health with the increase of honour I humbly take my leave from Virginia ...

Your honours to command

George Somers

A portrait of Sir George hangs in the Bermuda Historical Society Museum along with another of his wife. The authenticity of the portraits has been questioned. They were discovered by Lefroy late in the 19th century and were owned by descendants of Sir George, and the owner, who later sold them to Bermuda, declared that they were of Somers and his wife. When the portraits were cleaned some years ago it was discovered that they had been considerably retouched. A removal of the old paint revealed quite a different face from the familiar one which had hung on the walls for many years. Another portrait named 'George Somers' of quite a young man was found by the photographer John Weatherill and remains with its owners in England. Also in the Historical Society Museum is a lodestone (used to magnetize compass needles) and a chest. Sir George is also commemorated in Bermuda by a bronze statue by Mr Desmond Fountain erected on Ordnance Island, St George's. Mr Fountain depicts yet another face.

NOTE
1. Quoted in Lefroy, *Memorials*, Vol. 1, pp.10–11.

SOURCES
Lefroy, *Historye of the Bermudaes*.
Lefroy, *Memorials of the Bermuda*s.
Smith, *The Generall Historie of Virginia*, Vol. 1.
Weatherill, John, *The Bermudian*, Vol. 64, No. 5, May, 1993.
Wilkinson, Henry C., *The Adventurers of Bermuda* (2nd edition).

PART 2

The Archipelago

4

The First Beginnings

When Spanish sailors first found Bermuda jutting out of the broad expanses of the Atlantic the group of islands had already been in existence a long time. The story of the archipelago goes back 110 million years, when a volcano first formed. It was located, geologists believe, along a dividing line between two tectonic plates – two zones of harder surface rock. It remained on one of the plates – North America was on the same plate – and slowly moved westward with the American continent, so that the Bermuda volcano, once close to Europe, is now 3000 miles away. Thirty-five millions years ago, as it drifted, it came over a hot spot and there was a second eruption – enough to thrust up the mountain top to the sea surface.

As waves attacked the peak area above sea level, coral formations developed in the shallow waters around it, and from them came a carbonate sand which was blown over the diminished volcanic top, forming sand dunes. Rain falling on the sand caused a chemical action which turned it into limestone. The limestone cap, some 250 feet thick, entirely covers the volcanic rock.

The process by which the Bermuda of today came into being was long and arduous. The lowering of the ocean level, when ice locked up a large volume of the earth's water and Bermuda had 300 square miles of dry land, was complemented by warm periods when the world water level was much the same as it is today – and even times when the water level rose as much as 16 feet higher, drowning most of the island. The record of these changes is written in the caves and rocks, particularly in road and quarry cuttings which reveal strata of sand layered with hard stone, and layers of red earth sandwiched with stone. The earth is believed to have come from the Sahara Desert, and then, as trees and plants developed, enriched with compost from decomposing vegetation.

The formation of the Aeolian limestone rock of Bermuda is a continuous process, although obviously dune formation was accelerated during the ice ages when so much more of the surface was exposed. The process continues today, and can easily be seen taking place in a pile of sand left by itself, which develops a crust.

The stone is quite porous so that a layer of seawater permeates the rock horizontally and lies under the island. Rain permeates the rock vertically, and rests on the salt layer, making reservoirs of fresh water of the utmost importance in times of drought. Recent geological explorations of the freshwater 'lens' – thicker in the middle than at the edges – shows that the phenomenon does not occur everywhere but forms separate lakes contained in the pores of the stone.

The coral creatures are still at work today in this warm period, and dunes are still to be seen. During the late 19th century one sand-blown dune even covered a cottage in Paget in the Elbow Beach area. It seems likely that new sand is constantly being made by the reefs and the creatures that live there, and sand from the great western reef is moved by the frequent south-west winds along the South Shore, so there is always a fresh supply for the beaches when the older sand is moved right over the eastern edge of Mount Bermuda by heavy gales. It is only one of the important reasons for we Bermudians to do our best to preserve our coral reefs.

The hills created by the Elbow Beach dune are one of the small changes which have occurred since man came to Bermuda, but there are others. There is reason to think, for instance, that North Rock was much higher above sea level when Henry May was wrecked over 400 years ago. Under the water at Shelly Bay you can still the remains of a road which once ran across dry land.

The biggest change we know of, however, was man-made, in 1941, when the United States built an airfield at St David's, Cooper's and other islands. Sand was sucked up from the bottom of the sea, hills were torn down, and the land was massively reshaped into an airfield. The work produced clouds of sand in Castle Harbour and killed the coral, which is only now recovering.

Bermuda appears to have taken on its present appearance at the end of the last ice age of the Pleistocene. When the ice melted and the sea rose the valleys were drowned and only the higher hill-tops remained above the water. These were concentrated on the southern and western sides of the mountain top, leaving under water the shallow areas of the northern lagoon and the western reefs. Within the higher hills were three major basins: Great Sound, Castle Harbour and Harrington Sound. Some think the basins indicate the craters through which the ancient volcano once spewed its lava.

Offshore are two other lesser peaks, the Argus and Challenger Banks, which await the next ice age to reappear above the water.

Geography of Bermuda

The first mappers and explorers of Bermuda were struck by the large number of islands and islets, and it is still said today that the Bermuda archipelago, counting in a good many pinpoints of barely dry land, has 365 islands, one for every day of the year.

The major hills in Bermuda are found along the South Shore, running from Tucker's Town right onto Somerset Island. A lesser spine of hills goes along the North Shore, from Spanish Point along the northern edge of Harrington Sound, being picked up again on the northern side of St George's Island.

A surprising aspect of Bermuda is the number of caves, ranging in size from Crystal and Leamington caves to the small ones found all over the island. Several coves and valleys are caves whose roofs have collapsed. It is believed that the caverns formed slowly as softer rock was worn away by water. Then came the formation of drip rock, making many of the caves remarkably beautiful, with colourful shining stalactites hanging like icicles down from the roof and stalagmites working their way up from the floor.[1] These are formed by drops of rainwater seeping through the red soil and stone covering the roof. The drops pick up minute particles of material and leave some behind as they tinkle down to the floor. There more minute pieces of material are left, and slowly the stalagmites and stalactites grow toward each other as the drops form drip rock icicles and hillocks. The fact that stalactites and stalagmites can be seen under water, and that caves have been found well below sea level along the outer reefs on the South Shore, shows the way in which the ocean level has fluctuated over the millennia.

The Crystal Caves

Trees and Plants

Bermuda is a fertile island covered by vegetation, except where rock heads break through the soil. The trees, bushes and plants have changed considerably since the first man came, for ever since the island was settled men have introduced new species, and now Bermuda has a sampling of flora from many parts of the world. The subtropical climate supports more than 3000 species from cold and warm parts of the world, adding to the remarkable variety of trees and plants.

Because Bermuda is an isolated island over 600 miles from any other point of land, some varieties of trees and plants have developed which are found nowhere else. These endemic plants include the cedar, which once covered the island with a cool dark green forest. An insect pest which struck in the 1940s destroyed nearly all the trees. Whether these tough, hurricane resistant trees which can push their roots down through stone will ever dominate the island

One of the few remaining cedars

again is very questionable, but a marked comeback is under way, both natural and man-aided.

Another endemic is the olivewood bark, which fortunately is not now as rare as it was, many people and organizations – notably the Corporation of Hamilton – having taken the trouble to cultivate this lovely but slow-growing tree. Others are the Palmetto and the tiny Bermudiana, a little blue flower of the iris family which appears in the grass in the spring. Bermuda also has many native plants which were present when the first settlers arrived, having reached Bermuda as seeds floating on the ocean, borne on the wind or carried by birds.

A number of trees have sprung up or have been planted to take the place of the cedars. Prominent among the plants clothing the hillsides are the all-spice or pimento, whose leaves and seeds make a useful flavouring; the fiddlewood, whose leaves turn red in both autumn and spring; the Surinam cherry, whose red berries (which taste quite different from northern cherries) are a delight to children and adults, and can be used to make delicious jellies and jams; the equally pleasant and useful loquat from Japan; the tall Norfolk Island pine which stands out because of its height; and, among the palms, the hardy coconut and the column-like royal palm. There are two plants which have become a problem, and threaten to dominate the landscape. They are the Brazilian pepper, whose red seeds appear at Christmas time and seem to germinate everywhere with the greatest of ease, and the Chinese fan palm, which is very like the palmetto but which quietly kills any plants underneath it. A third tree, the Indian laurel, is a problem in a different way. Its seedlings cling to Bermuda's stone walls, spread powerful roots into any cracks, and gradually enlarge and damage their host. In the right surroundings the laurel grows rapidly into a very large and handsome tree, spreading tendrils down from its branches which, on reaching the ground, become auxiliary tree trunks.

Bermuda fruit trees include guavas, a wide variety of citrus and Canary Islands bananas. Although most people regard the *Bermudiana* as Bermuda's national flower, others would say that the queen of the Bermuda flowers is the Easter lily, Bermuda's last agricultural export and still to be seen in fields at Easter time. Common flowering shrubs throughout Bermuda are the oleander, often grown as a hedge, and the large hibiscus, which can be a shrub, a tree or a hedge plant. Morning glory or bluebell is a vine flower which grows cheerfully almost everywhere and is regarded as a pest, and in the spring Bermuda gardens rejoice in geraniums, narcissii, gladioli, statice, and many other species. On the seashore

Easter lilies: Bermuda's last export crop

can be found the wild prickly pear, with yellow flowers and a pleasant tasting red fruit, which must be peeled to get rid of the prickles before eating.

Ferns poke up in many places and include two common endemic varieties, the pretty maidenhair and the tough sword fern. The green grass of Bermuda is known to all Bermudians as crab grass, but in the United States it is called St Augustine grass.

Land Creatures and Birds

Bermuda has few wild animals, which is hardly surprising in view of the size of the archipelago. The largest are rats. Houses often have little lizards running through them, eating flies and insects. Most of the lizard species were imported, but one variety, the skink, is in fact an indigenous creature, but is rare and difficult to find.

Large saucer-shaped toads live in the fields and wander onto the roads. They were introduced to Bermuda by Captain Nathaniel Vesey in 1885 to help control pests. Bermuda also has two species of tiny whistling frogs, which arrived about the same time. The whistling frogs live in stone walls and in the bark of trees, and sing on summer nights and in the daytime after rain. Bermudians are used to it and barely hear them, but the noise is startling to visitors. The tale is told that the notable popular composer and singer John Lennon hired a house in Bermuda, and began to write and compose songs. He taped himself singing some, and sent these trial tapes to the United States to see whether others liked them. The songs were fine – but his friends were extremely puzzled at the strange whistling sound effect in the background.

Bermuda has never been inhabited by snakes. The only poisonous land creature is the centipede, which is rare. Centipedes are usually three to four inches long, equipped with a number of legs, and painful and poisonous pincers. Much more common are several varieties of spiders, butterflies, moths, houseflies and mosquitoes, although the flies and mosquitoes are nowadays far fewer in number than they were. Bermuda once suffered from *Aedes aegyptii*, the mosquito which is the carrier of yellow fever, but these were eliminated in a campaign which started during the Second World War.

One of the prettiest sights in a summer sky is the soaring black and white longtail or tropic bird sailing over the warm sea ready to dive into the water to catch a fish. The longtail is one of the few species of birds which regularly visit Bermuda. Another is the tiny warbler. Warbler flocks suddenly dominate the landscape for a few days before they take off again in their migratory passage.

A bird which is rarely seen and indeed is almost extinct is the cahow, which lived here in large numbers before man came to settle in Bermuda, and helped to feed the *Sea Venture* company. The rediscovery of cahows living on isolated islands in Castle Harbour, by Dr R. C. Murphy and Louis Mowbray in 1951, has led to a major and successful effort to increase the numbers of these wide-ranging sea birds, a difficult task as they only produce one egg a year. Dr David Wingate, Government Conservation Officer, has been in the forefront of the work, devising artificial burrows and working on means of excluding the cahow's enemies.

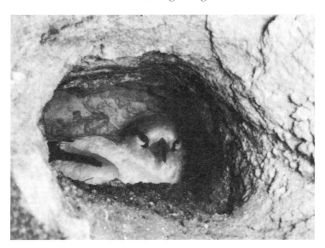

A longtail peers from its nest in the cliffs

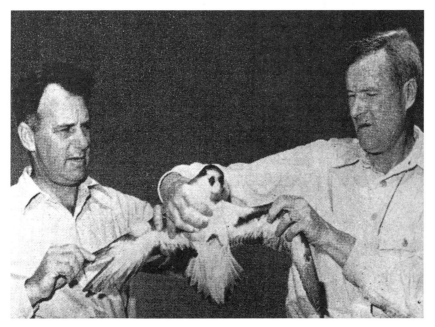

Rediscovery of the cahow

The principal island birds are the black cat bird, the yellow-breasted kiskadee, the European sparrow, the cardinal or redbird, the American crow, the tern, the white-eyed vireo, the ground dove, the starling and the pigeon.

Bermuda Sea Creatures

Silvanus Jourdan, in the first book published in England about the wreck of the *Sea Venture*, was ecstatic about the number of Bermuda fish. 'Sir George Summers,' he says,

> ... presently by his careful industry went and found out sufficient of many kinds of fishes, and so plentiful thereof that in half an hour he took so many fishes with hooks as did suffice the whole company one day. And fish there is so abundant that if a man step into the water they will come round about him, so that men were fain to get out for fear of biting. These fish were very fat and sweet, and of the proportion and bigness that three of them will conveniently lade two men; those we called rockfish.[2]

The fish are not so plentiful today and the Government has had to take steps to preserve fish stocks, primarily by forbidding the use of fishpots. These traps were designed so that when fish swam into them they could not find a way out. The traps worked well as a fishing tool if lifted every few days and emptied, but if left for longer periods or lost they simply starved the fish they trapped, and continued to kill fish for long periods. Decent fishermen added a door fastened with string which would fall open in time, but the species still diminished too fast. Today fishermen staying within the law use hook and line. Areas of water within the reef are closed to fishing during the summer.

In springtime humpback whales come to Bermuda waters to feed and raise their young before migrating further, and other species of whale pass by the island and occasionally become beached. Right up to the beginning of the 20th century whaling was a Bermuda industry, and old whaling implements and carvings from whale bones are still to be seen.

Bermuda fish are most easily divided into two sections: the inshore fish found round about the reefs and on the Argus and Challenger Banks, and the oceanic or pelagic fish which roam the Atlantic and are generally found in the deep ocean. Along the coast-

lines it is easy to find striped sergeant majors or cowpilots (pro-
nounced cowpollies), small, brightly coloured fish which are expert
at sneaking a bait off a hook. Also common are the grey bream
with a black dot on the tail, and the three species of small silver-
green fry which are much prized as bait. The fry often leap from the
water if pursued by enemies, particularly mackerels and jacks.
Grunts are also often seen (they make a grunting sound when
caught) in many species and differing colours. Harder to find are
the shy Angel fish. They are a deep blue colour, with bright yellow
fins and piping. Colourful parrot fish can often be seen by
snorkellers, and a favourite shallow water gamefish is the bonefish,
which can put up a good fight when hooked.

In deeper water are rockfish, varieties of snapper, hamlet,
grouper, mackerel and yellowtail. Also found are species of ray, the
dangerous-looking but gentle giants of the deep. Further out to sea
are the great Allison and blackfin tuna, dolphins and wahoo. The
principal hazard to swimmers is the presence of various species of
jellyfish, which sting, and the Portuguese man-of-war, which scien-
tists believe to be several individuals living together, the main one
the floating blue balloon, the long stinging tentacles being several
others. The tentacles deliver an intense sting which can produce a
dangerous shock, and the pretty balloons should be avoided.
Another hazard around coral reefs is red fire sponge and the ginger
coral which can give a painful rash.

Bigger creatures feared by many people are the varieties of
shark and barracuda (though the latter rarely attack humans).
Divers must watch for Moray eels which live in crevices in the rock.
They normally do not attack unless they feel cornered by a hand
going into a cranny – but if they do, their bite is severe.

NOTES
1. Memory aid: stalactites cling *tightly* to the roof.
2. Lefroy, *Memorials*, p.17.

SOURCES
Britton, *Flora of Bermuda*.
Iliffe, *The Bermuda Depths: A look at mid-ocean caves and caving*.

Lefroy, *Memorials of the Bermudas* (3rd edition).
Sterrer, *Bermuda's Marine Life*.
Sterrer, 'Bermuda's Shore Plants and Seaweeds'.
Sterrer, 'How Many Species are there in Bermuda?'
Sterrer, in cooperation with Christiane Schoepfer-Sterrer, *Marine Fauna and Flora of Bermuda*.
Wardman, *The Bermuda Jubilee Garden Book*.

5

The Sea and the Weather

Hurricane!

Far to the south of Bermuda a hurricane is spawning. Out in the Atlantic, not far north of the equator, some force causes hot air to rise from a low pressure area just above the surface of the water. As the upwind continues the pressure of the air on the earth lightens in that spot, and the low pressure area grows more intense. Because the atmosphere constantly tries to even the pressure, air rushes into the low pressure area or 'eye', and in its turn moves up the warm air column. The turning earth gradually creates a spinning motion and the small beginning can turn into an enormous storm.

The storm has winds which reach out for 200 miles or more. Clouds gather, and these are recorded by weather satellites circling the globe high above the atmosphere. The satellites send their signals to receiving stations and these convert the signals into maps showing the cloud cover over a vast area of the Atlantic – the sort of picture shown on television screens.

The circular nature of the hurricane makes it easy to spot, for its clouds look like a great spiral. Aircraft are sent to measure the storm and its intensity. By parachuting small radio devices into the walls of the low pressure eye, the men and women in the airplane receive news about the strength of the winds, and, according to their strength, classify the storm as a tropical disturbance, a tropical storm or, if the winds are over 75 mph, a fully fledged hurricane.

Thanks to modern warning systems there is usually time to prepare, to haul small boats up on land or to move them to safe anchorages, to shutter homes and buildings, and to evacuate when there is a danger of flooding. For Bermuda and the mid-Atlantic US states, normally distant from the spawning areas, it is a time of watching and waiting. A moving hurricane can go anywhere, and while forecasts have greatly improved in the decade of the 1990s, it is important to listen to predictions and be prepared – it is often useful to track a hurricane on one's own tracking map. Experience shows that when a hurricane starts east of Lesser Antilles, the eastern chain of islands which mark the boundary of the Caribbean Sea, and heads through or north of the Bahamas chain, there is a strong possibility of its coming near Bermuda. On the other hand a hurricane which hits Florida rarely comes close to the island.

Whether a hurricane will pass some distance away, brush us with gales, or make a direct hit with the eye passing right across the island, is unpredictable. Indeed, the hurricane patch described above is typical, but some hurricanes start in the Gulf of Mexico or even in the sea areas near Bermuda, giving very little warning of their approach.

But the more usual hurricane quickly develops great ocean waves which roll way ahead of the storm itself, covering an enormous area of ocean, and boom and crash on the South Shore, making an exciting display and tempting daring swimmers and windsurfers to pit themselves against the dangerous rollers. It is a thoroughly serious form of warning. Unlike areas further south, if sensible precautions are taken the heavy stone Bermuda walls will normally withstand the worst the storm can fling at them, and the heavy roofs, although more vulnerable, are also good at standing up to the fury of the storm. Eventually the storm passes, nearly always going north of Bermuda. When this happens it is likely to keep on going, usually dispersing as the water gets colder and the fuel for the great heat machine vanishes. Sometimes, however, it turns back, causing more worry. Occasionally the storm travels as far as Europe, causing damage as it smashes inland.

The hurricane is the most dramatic kind of weather Bermuda receives, but most of the time we are part of the general mid-Atlantic weather picture. In summer the middle of the North Atlantic is dominated by a great area of high pressure, and this is called the Bermuda-Azores high. The high helps Bermuda to have pleasant weather most of the summer months, with south-westerly breezes and sunshine mixed with quick rain squalls which can cause a heavy shower in one parish while a quarter of a mile down the road no rain falls at all.

In wintertime the Bermuda-Azores high tends to move south, and the character of the weather changes. Cold air sweeps out from the American continent over the Atlantic, and, although warmed as it passes over the Gulf Stream, brings colder temperatures to Bermuda. But the temperature never falls low enough to allow snow or ice – or almost never. The last time ice is said to have formed was in 1840, on Christmas Eve. Said the *Royal Gazette*:

> It will scarcely be credited – but such is the fact – that *ice* was formed on the low ground, in the neighbourhood of the marshes in various parts of these islands, but more particularly in the parishes of Warwick, Paget, Pembroke and Devonshire. We are assured by gentlemen of unquestionable veracity that in many places it was a full quarter of an inch thick ... ice forming in Bermuda is almost without precedent; such a thing has not occurred within the recollection of our oldest inhabitants.

Occasional hail squalls are exciting for children as the usually small lumps of ice plummet from the skies.

The Great Winter Shield

Bermuda winter weather is variable. Frequently the temperature is autumnal and the winds mild, but sometimes storms caused by the passage of weather fronts across the North Atlantic reach south as far as Bermuda. These are started by masses of polar air moving south across Canada and the United States, bringing blizzards to the continent. Intense low-pressure areas develop and sweep out into the Atlantic causing dangerous winter storms in the North Atlantic sea routes. The associated fronts sweep across the sea and if they reach far enough south bring powerful gale winds to Bermuda. This is the time that passing ships get into trouble, either being damaged by the heavy winds or waves, or running short of fuel in battling the storm.

The great winter shield for Bermuda is the Gulf Stream. The stream is a great current in the ocean, fed by the Equatorial current and the warm water of the Caribbean and the Gulf of Mexico.

It starts off in Florida and works it way north along the North American coast, finally swinging across the top of the globe south of Greenland and Iceland to bring warm water and air to England, Norway, Finland and even Russia. It makes a big difference: Bermuda is on the same latitude as Savannah, Georgia, which has occasional snow and ice; Great Britain is on the same latitude as Labrador and Hudson Bay where the winter is long, the sea frozen and the snowfall enormous, while the sea rarely freezes off the coast of the British Isles, the winters are about three months long, and heavy snowfalls are infrequent.

The other great oceanic fact which affects Bermuda is the Sargasso Sea which is roughly the water equivalent of the Bermuda-Azores high. The Sargasso Sea is an ocean area in the centre of the great circle of currents sweeping the North Atlantic, and the floating Sargasso weed grows in the sea in great patches.

Long before the Bermuda Triangle was invented there were ancient tales telling of ships caught by the weed and stuck in the Sargasso Sea for ever. It is true that hulks have been found in the

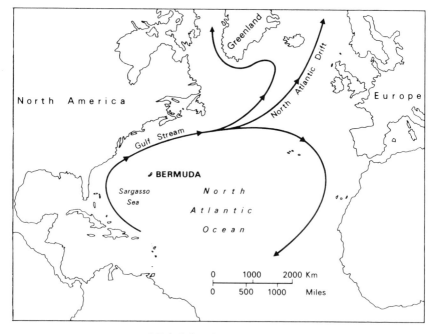

Mid-Atlantic sea currents

Sargasso, although today the most frequent objects are throw-away plastics which infest the Atlantic and often end up in the sea. Some wind up on Bermuda's shoreline. Thirty years ago there was a good deal of oil and tar as well: happily international action has nearly eliminated this pollutant, much of which came from tankers cleaning their tanks in mid-voyage.

The Sargasso weed also floats up on the island and is a welcome sight, for it is an excellent fertilizer. In the past it was placed directly on the fields; today farmers are urged to put it on a compost heap and let it rot down first.

The Water Problem

Bermuda has an average of 58 inches of rain a year, and usually needs every drop of it. The porous rock and soil means that there are no rivers or streams, and nearly all Bermuda houses have their own tanks or cisterns to store water caught on the roofs. If there is little rainfall the water stored in the tanks begins to run low, and while nowadays water trucks and government supplies have made a big difference, there are still anxious times for householders and farmers when little rain has fallen for six or eight weeks.

In recent years Bermuda's underground water storage has proved to be bigger than anyone thought. It was always known that a shallow well dug near the shore would produce fresh water, and that this was floating on top of the salt water. Much the same thing was known to be true around the marshes, which were used for watering cattle. After 1950 it was gradually realized that this fresh water could also be obtained in the centre of the island, and that here the amount of fresh water was likely to be greater. Geologists hired by the government have been able to pinpoint the extent of these reservoirs, and extraction of water is carefully controlled for fear that if the salt water level should rise the rock might become impregnated with salt and thus pollute the fresh water after the next heavy rain.

Whirlwinds, Waterspouts and Tornadoes

It is generally accepted that waterspouts at sea and tornadoes on land are the same phenomenon, and could well be dubbed 'whirlwinds' as Governor Benjamin Bennett did in the early 18th century. Bermuda is affected by whirlwinds from time to time, sometimes riding with a hurricane, as happened with Hurricane Emily which struck on 25 September 1987, or separately, as has occurred a number of times. Sometimes the whirlwinds come out of the dark, striking without warning, but sometimes on muggy days, usually in July or August, they can be seen trying to form over the ocean – grey tails working their way down from the clouds towards the sea.

When they come ashore they cause damage, but this is usually limited to a few houses. However, sometimes there are worse experiences. The whirlwinds riding on the wings of Hurricane Emily almost certainly caused a good percentage of the damage experienced that day, but apart from Emily there have been other whirlwinds not associated with hurricanes which have caused serious damage. One of them occurred on the evening of Easter Day, 5 April 1953. At least four whirlwinds swept across the island, sounding like chainsaws and lifting trees up into the air. Several houses were destroyed; in one, at Crawl, a young woman was killed as the roof fell in. One taxi driver had a narrow escape on Harrington Sound Road when his cab was lifted by one of the whirlwinds and deposited in the water. He managed to swim ashore. A parked car was put overboard at the same spot. Another serious tornado occurrence took place on 11 January 1986. A pair of whirlwinds swept over Smith's Parish and caused severe damage to St Mark's Church as well as to Verdmont, the historic house museum, and other buildings in the Harrington Hundreds and Knapton Hill area, while another whirlwind swept across St David's, damaging buildings and sinking boats at anchor.

SOURCES
Little, Wayne, & Bermuda Weather Service (oral communication).
Rushe, *Your Bermuda*.
Zuill, W.E.S., *Bermuda Sampler*.
Zuill, W.S., *St Mark's Church, A History*.

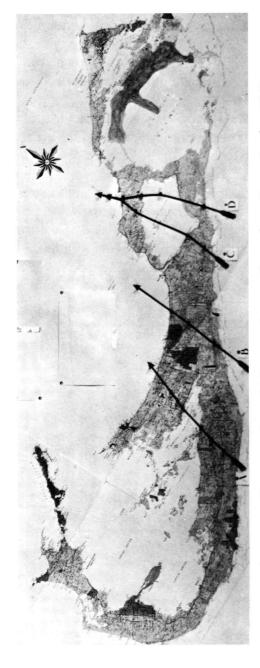

The routes of four tornadoes which stormed across Bermuda on Easter Sunday, 1953

PART 3

Story of the Bermuda People

6

Outline of Bermuda History

Christopher Carter was Bermuda's first settler, for he was the only member of the *Sea Venture*'s company who stayed on in Bermuda for most of his life (he made at least one trip to England) until he died in 1624. Thus human habitation of Bermuda started in 1609 but colonization of Bermuda did not begin until the arrival of the ship *Plough* in 1612 bringing English settlers, and the return to Bermuda from the West Indies of the ship *Edwin* in 1616 with an Indian and Negro on board. Thus ancestors of each of Bermuda's main races were on the island almost from the beginning.

The settlement was made by the Bermuda Company, and at first the community grew and flourished under their direction. It passed through difficult times during the English Civil War, and then Bermudians struggled to free themselves of the merchants ruling from London. The colony's first major political change occurred in 1684, when the Bermuda Company was wound up and Bermuda became a colony under the Crown.

A social change of much greater importance came 150 years later, in 1834, when slavery came to an end. Although Bermuda slavery in general was less harsh than slavery in most other places, there were serious cases of cruelty and torture which were part and parcel of laws which enabled one person to own another.

The other major political changes for Bermuda occurred in the 1960s, when every adult was given the right to vote, and when the British government surrendered its power to veto laws passed by the Bermuda legislature, reserving for itself only the right to oversee the colony in foreign affairs and in internal and external security.

The Economy

How did this small and isolated community survive? Bermuda might have developed into another Tristan da Cunha, an isolated island group in the South Atlantic where a very small community existed right up to recent times on fish and potatoes and very little else. Bermuda has done better than that, and in our own time has reached a very high standard of living, with more than sufficient wealth flowing in to provide nearly everyone with the material comforts of life. But it has not always been so, and throughout most of the 400 years of Bermuda's history the community has struggled to find ways of making a living. Thanks to the island's small size we have rarely been able to grow enough food for ourselves, and have had to find ways to pay for the food, clothing and comforts imported. It seems likely that the community went through many periods when rations were lean (an explanation for 18th century complaints that vegetables were hard to protect against theft). It is also interesting that most animal remains found by archaeologists exploring the cellars of 18th century buildings have been fish bones and rat bones (the former showing what people ate and the latter showing where the rats lived). Thus the

Hog money – the first coinage sent to Bermuda.
The design commemorates the hogs found by the
Sea Venture company

economy has been a constant factor in the life of the island, and our history falls into seven broad periods of distinct and differing major economic activities from the time of the first settlement to the present day, some of which were in progress at the same time.

Tobacco

The first economic period came soon after the early settlement of the island. People in Europe wanted tobacco, then a new discovery, and Bermuda, like Virginia, proved to have a good climate for growing it. Well before the end of the 17th century, however, Virginia had outstripped Bermuda in tobacco production and the Bermuda people turned to new trades which kept the community going until after 1800.

Cedar, Salt and Sailors

The second economic period, the time of cedar, salt and sailors, lasted into the 19th century. The forest of Bermuda cedar was turned into ships: small, fast sailing vessels, which roamed the western Atlantic in time of peace carrying goods from one port to another. In time of war many owners would obtain letters-of-marque, official commissions which made them an auxiliary navy with the power to capture enemy vessels, bring them into port and sell them. Without a letter-of-marque such captures would have been piracy.

The sailors were the black and white Bermudian crews who sailed the ships, facing the hazards of the sea far from home. The salt was the salt of the Turks Islands (two islands at the extreme eastern end of the Bahamas chain). The dry climate of these and other nearby islands was ideal for making salt out of sea water. Some salt-making occurred naturally, when sea water was washed up into natural rock pools, and the area appears to coincide with islands referred to in 18th century documents as the 'Saltertudos'. The salt was carried to the West Indies, the settlements up and down the eastern seaboard of the United States, and the Grand Banks. Nearly all our food today is kept from deteriorating by canning or refrigeration, but in the past food was dried or smoked, or preserved using salt or sugar. Salt meat laid down in casks enabled sailors to live for long periods at sea; salt fish meant that

*The Koh-I-Noor, built at the end of Bermuda's
ship-building era*

the produce of the teeming Grand Banks fishery could be shipped to
many parts of the world. So salt was a vital commodity, and its sale
enabled Bermudians to purchase food and necessities before sailing
for home.

With ships arriving from many parts of the western Atlantic,
Bermudians gained vital intelligence about what was needed where,
and where it could be found. This information enabled owners to
establish a successful carrying trade as well, purchasing goods in,
say, Charleston for transportation to Jamaica, and then picking up
a cargo in Kingston and taking it to Boston.

During the early 19th century these trades began to fail. The
cedar was almost entirely used up: pictures of the island at the time
show a landscape almost entirely without trees. Steam engines were
being installed in ships, and by the middle of the century steamships
were regarded as being as reliable as sailing vessels although most
carried auxiliary masts and sails. The ships themselves began to be
built with iron ribs, and later entirely of iron or steel. Some very

fine wooden vessels were built in Bermuda during the 19th century, but as an industry shipbuilding was nearly dead. Bermudians continued to find work as sailors, but less and less frequently on Bermuda-owned vessels.

In the late 18th century governance of the Turks Islands was placed in the hands first of the Governor of the Bahamas, and later of the Governor of Jamaica. Bermuda had lost control of the islands, although Bermudians continued to make salt.

British Base

Fortunately for Bermudians the strategic importance of the island increased. After the American Revolutionary War the Royal Navy could no longer have naval bases on the American mainland, and Bermuda, situated halfway between the major British base at Halifax and the Bahamas, became increasingly important.

During the 19th century Great Britain and the United States were often on bad terms, and after the war of 1812–14 there were several moments when fighting seemed imminent. After each of these crises Britain improved the British base, until today there are massive Victorian fortifications in many places. Fortifications meant building, soldiers stationed here, and work and income for Bermudians.

The last spurt of fortification in Bermuda ended in the early years of this century. The Royal Navy concentrated its forces in European waters to meet the threat posed by the new fleet being built by Kaiser Wilhelm II of Germany. In any case, by then relationships between Britain and the United States were generally good, and in 1917 were cemented even further when the United States entered the First World War on the side of Britain and her allies. Between the wars the good relations continued, and gradually the great British base here declined, until today, with the end of the Cold War, the British military presence has come to an end.

Potatoes and Onions

During the 19th century Bermudians revived agriculture and developed an excellent market in the northern United States in spring vegetables. The Agricultural Exhibition started at this time, and farmers competed with one another, as people still do today, keeping alive the feeling many Bermudians have for working the soil and growing their own vegetables and flowers. A number of events brought the agricultural period to an end. The discovery of a method of refrigeration for railroad boxcars meant that farmers in the southern United States could send their spring vegetables to New York and other cities which had formerly purchased from Bermuda, and at the same time increasingly harsh American customs duties on imported food pushed up the price of Bermuda vegetables. Gradually farming died, until now the remaining cultivated fields grow crops entirely for Bermuda's own consumption.

Tourist Trade

Even as the British base was being improved in the early years of the 20th century another industry was rising. In the late 19th century people came to believe that plenty of sunshine was good for the human body, and the steady improvement of steamships meant that Americans could come here easily during the hard winter to refresh themselves in the warmth of Bermuda's climate. Hotels were built and provided work and income for the islanders. It was a trend which was carefully nurtured and developed and today a great many Bermudians live in one way or another on the proceeds of the tourist business; indeed at the end of the 20th century, catering to tourists brings in half the community's overall income.

American Bases

Another important development came during the Second World War, when the United States, fearing that Britain might be overwhelmed by Hitler's Germany, obtained the right to build bases on Bermuda. These compensated for the economic loss resulting from the slow British withdrawal, and up to 1995, when the US Navy closed them down, they played an important part in Bermuda life. The airfield has been taken over by the Bermuda government and is used by civilian planes, while investigations continue into the use of other parts of the base. Bermuda already had some experience in this, having taken over the British imperial lands in the 1950s. A difficult problem was how to make use of the former British Dockyard, where it was hoped that light manufacturing would become an important economic activity. That was a partial failure, and the bulk of the property has turned into an interesting place to visit, attracting both tourists and Bermudians.

Offshore or Exempted Companies

The most recent economic change has been the discovery, principally by British, American and Canadian companies, that Bermuda is a good place from which to operate. At first the main reason was heavy taxation in the home countries, but there have been other considerations as well, such as complicated laws governing company operations in other places. The growth of this business in Bermuda has resulted in increasing numbers of jobs being available in clerical fields requiring skills in shorthand, typing and accounting, and Bermudians are becoming increasingly competent in this kind of work. Today the companies, which are exempt from some Bermuda laws, bring in as much income as tourism. The life of Bermudians has been constantly governed by these economic factors, and our skills and folk memories look back to the things our forefathers had to do to stay alive. In the future we may have to learn new ways to keep this small and isolated community going.

The Bounty of the Deep

Fishing and whaling were never vital to Bermuda's economy, but both were important to individuals. Fishing, particularly, has been a sport and a business throughout Bermuda's story; whaling started in the 17th century and was only discontinued in the early years of this century.

Whaling was exciting and dangerous. When the whale's spout was seen, boats would be manned and the chase would start. When the boat was close enough the harpooner threw his harpoon into the whale, which usually reacted wildly, diving deep or swimming at great speed, hauling the boat behind it. Eventually the whale tired and the whalers could come close and attack it with lances until it died. Then it was pulled to shore, the fatty blubber cut off and cooked in large iron pots until it turned to oil. The whale meat was eaten and the bone used for a variety of purposes. The most famous Bermuda tale about whaling occurred in the 20th century.

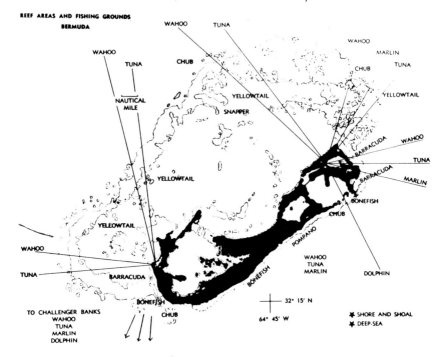

*Map of the main reef areas and fishing grounds,
published by the Department of Tourism*

In St David's, the story goes, a number of people had doubts about the Biblical account of the prophet Jonah's being swallowed by a whale and later coughed up. The whale's stomach, they said, was too small. Tommy Fox, a notable personality on the island, said the doubters were wrong, and the next time a whale was caught he worked his way down into the stomach. He declared it was a 'considerable apartment'.

Sport fishing as opposed to fishing for food has become a highly developed pastime in the last 75 years as motorboats have replaced sailing vessels. Today the fishing guides compete in economic importance with the men who sell their catch to hotels, restaurants and the general public – and indeed when the sport fishing boat returns to the dock the day's catch is usually sold for eating. Fish are important to scuba diving businesses as well, as part of the underwater landscape which clients expect to see. They also contribute to the stability of the coral growth on the reefs.

The dangers of whaling (reconstruction)

Therefore commercial fishing is carefully regulated, and after a serious decline fish stocks appear to be recovering. Bermuda received a large addition to the area under its economic control when, through international treaties, it gained exclusive fishing rights to a vast circle of ocean stretching 200 miles from its shores – a third of the distance to Cape Hatteras, the nearest point of land. Bermuda's territorial waters also increased from three miles offshore to 12 miles. These changes stimulated fresh interest in deep ocean fishing and spurred the Government to purchase a fisheries research vessel.

7

The First Settlers

By 1612 Edward Chard, Christopher Carter and Robert Waters were alone on the island. Matthew Somers had sailed away in the *Patience* and the three of them, at the suggestion of Carter, had agreed to stay behind. They must have thought that another ship would come to Bermuda soon, but in fact two long, lonely years stretched ahead of them.

One day Chard was walking along the seashore. He was looking for anything he could pick up that might be useful – and then he spotted a large lump of a grey, waxy substance. Having some knowledge of the sea and its curiosities, he went over to it, and, as he thought, it was ambergris. Ambergris was then, and still is, in some processes, a major ingredient in making perfume. It comes from sick whales and was and is very rare. In the coinage of the early 17th century it was worth three English pounds an ounce in London, and so even a small piece was a considerable treasure. The lump found by Chard weighed 80 pounds, and there were other small lumps beside. He ran to tell Carter and Waters, and the three of them heaved the ambergris away from the shore and into a hiding place.

Until now the three men had lived peacefully together, but the ambergris changed that. Chard and Waters, particularly, each longed to have sole possession of the treasure, and the silent hills re-echoed to the noise of threats and quarrels. Carter, who was an easy-going man, hid all the weapons because he was afraid of being left alone on Bermuda. Time, and the solitude and peace of the island, gradually worked on Chard and Waters, and they saw the stupidity of their behaviour. They patched up a peace between them, and then all three, at Waters' suggestion, started work on a boat to take them to Virginia or Newfoundland – but before they made much progress a ship entered St George's harbour.

Arrival of English Settlers

It was the *Plough*, and aboard were fifty settlers and the first Governor, Richard Moore. The ship anchored off an island which they called Smith's Island in honour of Sir Thomas Smith, one of the principal shareholders of the Virginia Company. The three men made contact with them, and shortly afterwards the company moved over to the larger island which they called St George's. Governor Moore questioned Chard about any discoveries the three men had made, but Chard kept quiet about the ambergris. Shortly afterwards he, Waters and Carter tried to bargain with Captain Davis of the *Plough* to take the ambergris to England privately.

Carter mulled the matter over in his mind, and decided to tell Moore. The Governor seized the ambergris, imprisoned Chard, reproved the others in the plot, and decided to send the ambergris to England a portion at a time. No doubt he felt that sending portions would keep the Virginia Company interested in Bermuda, but at the same time he was not risking the whole amount in one ship – particularly one with Captain Davis as captain, for at one point Davis threatened to land his sailors and seize the ambergris, and the settlers had to be put on guard.

Chard and Waters eventually emigrated to Virginia, for Chard was released after Moore left, but Carter stayed in Bermuda for most of the rest of his life. He must have gone to England at one point for there is a record of his return. He was offered St David's Island as a reward for revealing the plot, but picked Cooper's Island (now part of the airfield) instead. He thought treasure was buried there, but never found any.

Defence of Bermuda

The Spanish were not pleased that people of other European countries were settling in the western hemisphere. The Pope had divided the world outside of Europe between Spain and Portugal, and the

Spanish did not accept any other settlements. Guns at Jamestown were pointed down the river in case the Spanish arrived, and some saw Bermuda as an outpost of Virginia. Governor Moore quickly started creating defences for the new colony. He was a carpenter by trade, and an able one, and the forts went up quickly.

It was good that he did so – in Madrid the King of Spain and his advisers considered plan after plan for capturing Bermuda, for even though there was peace between England and Spain in Europe, the Spanish did not accept that it extended to the western Atlantic. Bermuda was a particular concern because Spanish ships laden with the wealth of South America passed close by on their way home. Fortunately for Moore and the settlers the King and his Council could never make up their minds, but in 1614 Captain Domingo de Ulivari, bound for Spain in company with another ship, decided to make a reconnaissance. His ships sailed in towards Castle Harbour, but smoke signals gave the alarm to the Governor and he hurried over to his newly built fort at Castle Island, ready for the emergency which he had foreseen. Moore and the garrison had only one cannon which was working. The Governor carefully sighted the gun and fired it. The round cannon ball went over the mast of the leading ship. Hastily reloading the gun, the Governor took aim again, and this time succeeded in sending a ball whistling through the ship's rigging.

It was enough. The Spanish, who were handicapped by having a boat out taking soundings to guide the vessels, turned about and set out to sea. The Governor and his men breathed a sigh of relief. They only had one cannon ball left, and the gunpowder had been spilled out of its cask.

Governor Moore under Attack

Hard as the Governor laboured (there is reason to think that he even made the handsome altar table at St Peter's Church), the settlers were by no means content, and sent adverse reports about him back to London. By this time a number of shareholders of the Virginia Company had purchased Bermuda for £2000, and the island was now under the control of the Bermuda or Somers Island Company. The shareholders were unhappy because no more ambergris had been found, and there was no abundance of pearls; in

Governor Moore's defence against the Spaniards (reconstruction)

short, they had paid out money and received little in return. The blame was falling on the Governor's shoulders, so Moore decided to return to Britain to defend himself.

He left Bermuda in the control of six men, each one of whom was to be Governor for a month. It is known as the time of the Six Governors, and it was an odd period with one man setting the island by its ears, another leaving on a piratical expedition, and others, like Christopher Carter, taking it easy and letting others do so to. It is said of Carter's month: 'Not a hoe, axe, pickaxe or shovel was so much as once heard in the streets, nor an oar seen or heard unless when their stout stomachs compelled them to it.'

Governor Daniel Tucker

Word eventually reached London, and the company decided to send out someone who could do something about the situation. They picked Daniel Tucker, who owned a plantation in Virginia and had a reputation of being a strong man. His reputation was well deserved. Governor Tucker, who is still celebrated in the United States in the folk song ' Ole Dan Tucker', quickly changed the 'perpetual Christmas' which reports in London had spoken about. He did not hesitate to use the lash to enforce his commands, one man even being hanged for speaking against him, and soon the settlers were hard at work – if not happy.

One group, led by Richard Saunders, suggested they should build a good-sized boat for the Governor to fish in, no matter how bad the weather. The Governor agreed to what he thought was a kind offer, the men cleared off to a distant part of the island, and built the boat. When Governor Tucker went to fetch it he found the men had sailed away in it. After a long and hazardous voyage the runaways finally made landfall at Ireland, 3500 miles away.

Saunders' adventures were not over. He soon afterwards set sail for the East Indies, where he happened to buy a locked chest for three or four shillings. No key could be found and Sanders was sorry he had spent the money. One day, having nothing else to do, he forced the lock – and found $1000 inside.

Governor Tucker sailed to Bermuda on a ship called the *George*, accompanied by another called the *Edwin*, which was sent to the West Indies. In 1616, soon after the Sanders group had stolen away, she returned to Bermuda. Aboard her were two men who became Bermuda's first black and Indian settlers. Their names are not recorded, but they were not necessarily slaves. The Somers Island Company had authorized Governor Tucker to bring in black people as divers, and during a trial of this period a black man was sentenced to become a slave during the Governor's pleasure. His name, the first black person's name to be recorded, was given as Symon the Negro.

Other black persons came from England as tropical agricultural specialists. They are noted particularly in the *Rich Papers*, a compilation of early letters from Bermuda. An anecdote from the papers tells of Robert Rich, a member of the powerful Earl of Warwick's family and their representative in Bermuda, being arrested by Governor Tucker on information given by Christopher Carter. Tucker sentenced Rich to be hung – then rescinded his sentence at the last moment, probably thinking that the Rich family would never forgive him if Rich were executed.

One of Governor Tucker's biggest problems was an invasion of rats. Back in 1614 they had landed from a ship which brought meal, and by 1616 they had infested most of Bermuda. It was a plague which neither dogs, cats nor traps seemed able to combat, but soon after Governor Tucker left, many of the rats disappeared during a particularly severe winter. Burnt House Hill in Warwick is supposed to be named after this period, for an attempt was made to kill off the rats, some of which nested in trees, by burning great sections of land, and Burnt House Hill is possibly one of the areas burnt.

Norwood's Survey

During Tucker's administration Bermuda was first properly surveyed by a remarkable man named Richard Norwood. Norwood, an able mathematician, first came to Bermuda to look for pearls. He achieved some fame in England by using a crude diving device called a diving bell to salvage guns from a sunken ship and the Somers Island Company directors thought the technology would be useful in pearl diving. He had little chance to carry out this work during the time of the Six Governors (when he lived in a cave), and Tucker arrived and gave him the job of surveying the island. Norwood's diving bell, however, may have inspired Bermuda sailors, for in later years Bermudians became noted for their diving bells.

Norwood's survey was remarkably accurate, and has stood the test of time right up to the present. It was he who divided Bermuda into eight *tribes* (now parishes) and the public land at St George's. He made one mistake in dividing the land and thus ended up with a surplus between Southampton and Sandys. This became known as the Overplus (today there is an Overplus Lane) and the Governor seized it as a personal award for himself. Tucker had many enemies in Bermuda by now, and this last move led several of them to complain to London. Some months afterwards the Governor was advised to return to London to defend himself, which he did, opening the way for one of Bermuda's finest Governors, Nathaniel Butler. In London Tucker was reproved for his land grab, but allowed to keep a portion of the Overplus. Later he returned to Bermuda to live.

Names of a number of the earliest settlers who arrived here during the first fifteen years still crop up in Bermuda today, either as family names or place names. Table 1 (page 70) lists some of them. Spellings may have changed somewhat over the passage of time.

SOURCES
Craven, *An Introduction to the History of Bermuda*.
Harris, *Bermuda Forts*.
Ives, *The Rich Papers, Letters from Bermuda*.
Lefroy, *Historye of the Bermudaes*.
Lefroy, *Memorials of the Bermudas* (3rd edition).
Smith, *The Generall Historie of Virginia*.
Wilkinson, *The Adventurers of Bermuda* (2nd edition).

Table 1   Bermuda Names

Abbott, Adams, Allen, Amorie, Atwood
Baker, Ball, Barrett, Bassett, Beake, Bell, Bosse, Bostock, Brangman,
     Brown, Burgess, Burrows
Cann, Carter, Chamberlain, Clarke, Cooke, Cooper, Cox
Davis, Deane, Dunscombe
Edmunds, Ely, Evans
Fludd, Foord, Frith
Green, Guin (later Gwynne?)
Hall, Harford, Harman, Harriott, Harris, Harrison, Harvey,
     Hayward, Higgs, Hill, Hinson, Hughes
Joell, Johnson, Jones
Kempthorne
Lambert, Lea, Lewis, Llewellyn, Lucroft (later Leycroft?), Lunne
Middleton, Miller, Milles, Milner, Mitchell, Morgan, Morris Nash,
     Newman, Norwood
Outerbridge
Palmer, Parker, Paynter, Peniston, Perinchief, Pitman, Pitt, Plaice,
     Powell Reynor, Richardson, Roberts, Robinson
Scott, Scroggan, Seymour, Sears, Smith, Stafford, Stevens, Stokes,
     Stowes, Symonds, Swan
Tatem, Trimingham, Trott, Tucker
Vaughn
Walker, Warde, Washington, Watlington, Webb, Welch, Welman,
     West, Wilkinson, Williams, Wilson, Wiseman, Wood
Younge

8

The Company's Great Gift

The Bermuda Company soon gave pain and trouble to the early settlers. The Company gave instructions from London about small details of life in the island and tried to keep all the trade going in and out of Bermuda in its own hands – indeed, the very existence of the Company prolonged island troubles.

For all that the Company gave one great gift to Bermuda – a parliament. Its powers were limited but at its meetings representatives of the settlers could put their point of view and know that they would have a hearing. It was a parliament which gave trouble to Governors and to the Company and then to the British Government; it was often slow in its workings, but it endured and gave the Bermuda people a representative institution throughout the long history of the island. Bermudians gained a great deal from it, and it helped bring the island through many difficult times. Today the parliament has greater powers than ever before, but that is a recent change.

Governor Nathaniel Butler

The parliament ordered by the Company was instituted by Governor Nathaniel Butler who succeeded Governor Tucker. Butler stands out among Governors not just because he instituted Parliament, but also because of his intelligence, ability and energy: qualities he was going to need in Bermuda. He also wrote the first history of Bermuda (the *History of the Bermudaes*) which seems to have been used by Captain John Smith in the Bermuda chapter of his *General Historie of Virginia*.

Butler faced a crisis the first day he arrived. He sailed in aboard the ship *Warwick* and the acting Governor, Miles Kendall, came out to greet him. Butler invited Kendall, his councillors and the island's only clergyman, the Rev. Lewes Hughes, to dinner on the ship, which was anchored in Castle Harbour not far from Castle Island. Suddenly flames burst from the castle, and everyone was forced to hurry ashore to fight the fire, which did a great deal of damage.

So one of Butler's first jobs was to repair the fort. Then further trouble beset the colony when a tremendous hurricane hit Bermuda, damaging many houses and sinking the *Warwick*. The problem of finding cannon Governor Butler solved by raising guns from the *Warwick* and later from the *Sea Venture*. Perhaps he used the diving bell Norwood had invented. The Governor waited until the new St Peter's Church had been completed before he summoned representatives to meet there for the first parliament on 1 August 1620. It was a momentous occasion, and Governor Butler gave a superb speech, parts of which hold good to this day:

> Thanks be to God, that we are thus met, to so good an end as the making of good and wholesome laws; and I hope the blessed effect will manifest that this course was inspired from heaven into the hearts of the undertakers in England (shareholders in the Bermuda Company) to pronounce and offer it unto us, for the singular good and welfare of this plantation ...
>
> Take due notice that we come not hither for ourselves only and to serve our turns, or any man else's in particular, but to serve and regard the public. We are, therefore, to rid ourselves of all base desires of gain; we are to despise all private interests, thus afar at least, as to cause them to give way to the general.
>
> It may well be that some men chosen to be burgesses [members of the House of Assembly] here may find some bills preferred into this Assembly that may strike at some getting and income of theirs in particular. If they do so, let them remember their oaths, let them not shame themselves, and the place they hold here ... If, in their own consciences, they find that hitherto they have done injury to a common good, let them not augment it by obstinacy ... I grant there is a freedom of speech and opinion with modesty to be held by every man here ... .

Let us beseech God to inspire us with peaceable spirits, and such thoughts and desires as become honest, loyal and wise men, such as may be for his glory and the forming of this hopeful and forward plantation ... .[1]

Although the first meeting of the House of Assembly was held in St Peter's Church, Governor Butler also intended to build a house where Parliament could meet and where the courts could be held. In doing so he created a building which in many ways gave a lead to the traditional Bermuda house. It was Butler's second stone building in Bermuda – the first was erected on Castle Island of 'hewen stone'. The one-and-a-half storey State House had thick walls to withstand hurricanes, small windows to keep out the hot sun and a flat roof because buildings in the warm Mediterranean had flat roofs. This latter feature was a mistake, for the roof leaked, and was eventually replaced with a normal pitched roof. The State House was restored in time for the 350th anniversary of the first parliament in 1970, and now looks like the building illustrated in Smith's *Generall Historie of Virginia* – the roof is flat once again. Presumably the State House was completed before October 1622 when Butler sailed for Virginia to inspect that colony before he returned to England.

The Civil War

There were troubles in the colonies, but worse trouble was brewing in England. Varying religious beliefs were at the root of much of the discord. The Protestant Reformation in Europe had ended the complete power of the Roman Catholic Church, and led to the development of many new ideas about how God wished people to worship. The supporters of each idea believed that their way of worshipping God was the right and true way, and that it was their Christian duty to oppose, in battle if necessary, those who supported different methods of worship. Seventeenth-century Europe suffered from several religious wars. Britain was affected by the clash of religious ideas. The country had become officially Protestant in the 16th century, when the Church of England was set up. There still were Roman Catholics but they were regarded with great suspicion by most of the population.

Some of the more extreme Protestants became known as Puritans, who, as their name suggests, wanted the worship of God to have a simple purity. Queen Elizabeth I managed to keep an uneasy peace between religious groups, giving the Church of England her own support. Her successor, King James I, who was not such a strong ruler, found it much more difficult to control the religious pressures.

The situation worsened even further when his son, King Charles I, married a Roman Catholic, showed sympathy towards Roman Catholics, and appointed a man of similar views, William Laud, as Archbishop of Canterbury (the most important position in the Church of England). Archbishop Laud not only tried to make the service of the Church of England more elaborate but he also started a campaign against the Puritans, fining or imprisoning them. Many of them sailed across the Atlantic to start the colonies in New England where they could worship as they wished.

King Charles still had plenty of enemies left in England. There were many who disliked his religious views, and who bitterly opposed the way he ruled the country in general. This discontent was expressed by Parliament and the situation eventually grew so bad that a civil war started, with the King and his supporters on one side and Parliament and its supporters on the other. The war finally ended with the defeat and execution of the King.

In Bermuda the Puritans, known as Independents, were very powerful. Many of them had left England to escape persecution but their rule in Bermuda was oppressive and intolerant. One of those who suffered from their intolerance was Richard Norwood who had returned to Bermuda as schoolmaster in 1638. He spoke out against the Independents and as a result was forced out of his job.

In 1646 Governor Josias Forster (whose chair is now the throne chair in the Legislative Council chamber) allowed the Puritan ministers to have the upper hand because he was powerless to do otherwise, but he was soon replaced from London by Governor Thomas Turner. Turner called a meeting of the House of Assembly, which turned out to be entirely anti-Puritan. The Assembly forbade the holding of Puritan services, and the Independents complained to the Bermuda Company, whose headquarters were in London – which, throughout the Civil War, was dominated by Parliamentary forces. In response to the Puritans' complaints the Company sent out an

Ducking stool being used to punish an erring wife at the time of the Independents (reconstruction)

instruction that Norwood should be Governor, assisted by William Wilkinson (a Puritan) and Captain Christopher Leacraft who, unknown to the Company, had died.

When the orders reached Bermuda there was an immediate uproar, for Norwood was felt to be too friendly to the Independents even though he had quarrelled with them, and a demonstration at St Peter's Church prevented him from reading himself in as Governor. Norwood was not anxious for a fight, so he declined to serve, and the people of Bermuda would not accept Wilkinson as Governor.

Faced with this situation the Council in Bermuda restored Governor Turner, but some months later the news was received that King Charles had been executed in London. This horrified most of the settlers, and soon the anti-Puritans called out the militia. The militia, headed by John Trimingham, called themselves 'the Army' and marched on St George's. There they ensured that Governor Turner and his Council declare their allegiance to the Prince of Wales, the future King Charles II, and then they put Turner out of office and replaced him with Trimingham. It was in effect a miniature civil war. The anti-Puritans put pressure on the Independents to leave Bermuda, and some of them went to the Bahamas and some to other West Indian Islands. There are still surnames in the Bahamas which are the same as those held by Bermudians.

The following year the Company in London, more confident of its authority now that England was unified under the power of Oliver Cromwell, replaced Trimingham with Josias Forster, and the civil war, the only one in Bermuda's history, was over. Things ran more quietly in Bermuda during the remainder of Cromwell's period of rule, known as the Commonwealth, but when King Charles II was restored to the throne in 1660, Bermudians were quick to give him allegiance.

Norwood's Second Survey

After the Restoration Norwood started his second survey of Bermuda, and it is on this survey that the landholdings in Bermuda were based. Norwood's method of running his property dividing lines straight across the island from the South Shore to the North Shore (probably so that the shares would contain good land and bad) still leaves its mark on Bermuda. There are old stone walls

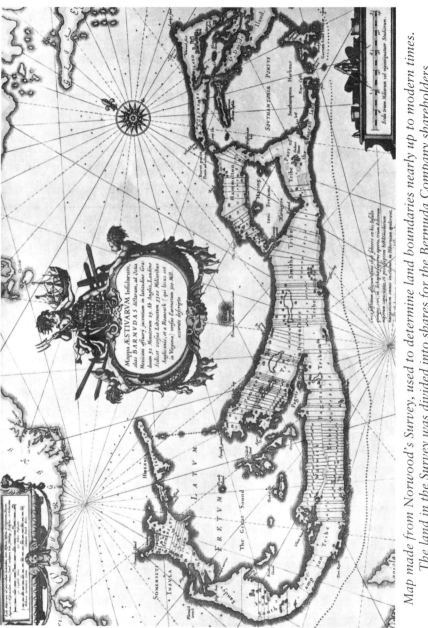

Map made from Norwood's Survey, used to determine land boundaries nearly up to modern times.
The land in the Survey was divided into shares for the Bermuda Company shareholders

77

which march in straight lines up and down hill, and aerial photographs of Bermuda show even more clearly this cross-island alignment.

More about Butler

In Bermuda Governor Butler is remembered mainly as an able administrator, but he was also a writer and warrior. After leaving Bermuda he went to Virginia on behalf of the Earl of Warwick to make a report on that colony, which had just suffered an Indian war in which large numbers of settlers had been killed. Many died in the Indians' initial surprise attack in 1622 which has often been called a massacre. While in Virginia he took part in a campaign against the Indians, and then he returned to England where he wrote a book called *The Unmasking of Virginia*. The Virginia Company was already in trouble, and this book helped to bring about its downfall, which finally occurred in 1624.

He probably wrote his book about Bermuda at the same time, but it was not published until 1882 when the manuscript, owned by the British Museum, was rediscovered by Governor Lefroy, who thought it was written by Captain John Smith. Since then scholars have uncovered convincing evidence that it was by Butler. Reading between the lines, it seems likely that much information came to Butler from Christopher Carter.

Soon after returning to England Butler was appointed to command a ship in an expedition which tried to capture the Isle of Re near La Rochelle on the Bay of Biscay coast of France. Then he undertook a more exciting job. In 1630 a group of Puritans, anxious to harm Spain, decided to settle on an island deep in the Caribbean off the coast of what is now Nicaragua, right in the centre of the Spanish possessions. At first the settlement, known as Providence Island, was run on peaceful lines, but in the late 1630s the Spanish attacked. They were defeated, but the Providence Adventurers in London decided they would take strong measures to prevent further trouble. The most important of these measures was the appointment of Butler as Governor.

Butler quickly gathered a fleet of English and Dutch privateers and attacked the town of Truxillo capturing 16 000 pieces of eight (Spanish dollars) from it; Butler sailed back to England with the loot, but after he had gone the enraged Spanish attacked Providence, failed to capture it, tried again and in May 1641, succeeded.

NOTE
1. Quoted in Lefroy, *Historye of the Bermudaes*, pp.194–7.

SOURCES
Craven, *An Introduction to the History of Bermuda*.
Harris, *Bermuda Forts*.
Ives, *The Rich Papers, Letters from Bermuda*.
Lefroy, *Historye of the Bermudaes (thought to be by Nathaniel Butler)*.
Lefroy, *Memorials of the Bermudas* (3rd edition).
Smith, *The Generall Historie of Virginia*.
Wilkinson, *The Adventurers of Bermuda* (2nd edition).

9

Salt and Pirates

Charles II was in a quandary – how was he going to establish royal rule more firmly? It was important so that the next Monarch – probably his brother James – could safely mount the throne and run the country without the danger of another Parliamentary revolt. The answer, he thought, was to make sure that a majority of the powerful House of Commons was made up of friends of the King. A great many members of the Commons were elected by the officials of the towns and cities of England, and these boroughs all had Royal charters. If the charters were changed the officials could be changed, and if the officials were friends of the Stuarts then they would send friends of the Stuarts to London to sit in Parliament.

So the King's lawyers began a studied assault on the boroughs through a legal process known as *quo warranto*, and the borough charters were brought down and replaced with new ones. This led a group of Bermudians in London to think that the same process could be applied against the Bermuda Company, which no longer attracted distinguished and able persons to run its affairs, but was in the hands of a few avaricious merchants who held their meetings in London and thus ruled over a community 3000 miles away which included the majority of the shareholders. There was constant trouble between these merchants and the Bermudians. Among other problems was that harvests of the staple crop of tobacco were uncertain as Bermuda's fields were exhausted of nutrients, and the island could not compete with Virginia where thousands of acres were under cultivation. One of the Bermuda Company's last major customers was the Hudson Bay Company.

The King's lawyers were glad to oblige, and the Bermuda Company lost its charter in a courtroom in London in 1684. Bermuda was now a royal colony, governed directly by the British government. The Bermudians were delighted to be free of the Company's restrictive practices, although they disliked the first thing that happened, the appointment of Colonel Richard Coney, the last company Governor, as the first Royal Governor.

The Bermudian example was noted by an active and intelligent official in Boston named Edward Randolph. Randolph suggested that the same process might bring down the Massachusetts charter, for the Crown found the Massachusetts Bay Company disobedient and troublesome. The process was used successfully, and soon charters of other New England colonies were removed as well. Unlike the Bermudians, the New Englanders hated the change.

In Bermuda Coney faced implacable enemies. No doubt a number of important people had expressed themselves with appalling frankness, expecting to see Coney go. By now James II was on the throne of England, and although many regretted that this was so, James' army was able to defeat a revolt led by the Duke of Monmouth, an illegitimate son of Charles II. News of the revolt, but not of its failure, reached Bermuda and Coney's enemies decided to take action. They seized several forts, but just then the remarkable treasure hunter William Phipps (see below), a New Englander, sailed in to Bermuda and took Coney's side. Phipps had to go on to England, but then a pirate, Bartholemew Sharpe, appeared, a man with a remarkable record. He fought the Spanish in the Pacific and sailed a battered Spanish ship around Cape Horn. He returned to England and was put on trial but was found not guilty of piracy. The gift to the Crown of a captured secret Spanish pilot book, which gave directions for sailing into the Spanish harbours of South America, led to his being commissioned in the Royal Navy. Instead of taking up his post he returned to piracy, then sought legitimacy through a commission granted by the Governor of Nevis.

Sharpe saved Coney, who was finally able to re-establish his administration when a Royal Navy frigate arrived. Sharpe was arrested, taken to Nevis and tried, but once again his luck was in, and he was found not guilty, partly because of the praise Coney heaped upon him.

It was a time of economic transition for Bermuda, and the islanders turned away from tobacco. The sea was calling, the cedar was waiting to be turned into ships, and down to the south there was an important and valuable crop to be gathered: salt.

The Salt Trade

It was in 1678 that Bermudians first sailed south to the Turks Islands, six years before the end of the company. They soon realized the possibilities of trading in salt; it was a precious commodity

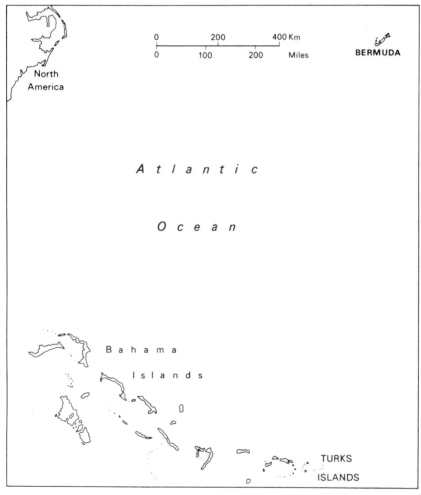

Bermuda and the Turks Islands

before the days of refrigeration when it was the principal ingredient in the preserving process for fish and meat.

For fourteen years they made salt in peace, pumping water into settling ponds, waiting for the sun to evaporate the water, and raking up the salt. In 1692, however, they faced a new and more energetic Governor in the Bahamas: he was actually a Bermudian named Nicholas Trott, whose family had played a major role in bringing the Bermuda Company to an end. Under orders from the English courtiers who at that point owned the Bahamas, he started levying taxes on salt exports from the Turks Islands. The Bermudians, who thought the Bahamas had no right to do this, protested bitterly in London, but things became even worse in the early 18th century when Bermuda ships were seized by the new Governor of the Bahamas, Elias Haskett, and sold. It was Haskett who once said he had never hanged a Bermudian, 'but would make no more to do it than to hang a dog'.

Not surprisingly, there was almost war between Bermuda and the Bahamas. Haskett and his friends were racketeers, and in Bermuda Governor Benjamin Bennett gave Bermudians letters-of-marque so that they could act against these enemies. It turned out that the Bahamians could not stand Haskett either, and they turned him out of office and shipped him to New York.

Worse problems were to come for Bermudians and Bahamians alike. With the death of the childless King of Spain fighting broke out between claimants for his throne, with Britain, Holland and Austria on one side and France and some factions in Spain on the other. For Bermuda the War of the Spanish Succession (Queen Anne's War) meant keeping men at home in case of invasion, rather than letting them go to sea, a sensible precaution as the Turks Islands and New Providence were attacked by the French and Spanish who captured both. It was in 1706 that Bermuda lost the Turks Islands: they were recaptured four years later by Captain Lewis Middleton and the crew of the Bermuda privateer *Rose*.

It was a long war, and when peace came in 1713, there was little peace at sea. Men who had served in privateers, or in the navies of the warring nations, found themselves bereft of the only life they had known. Various circumstances led them to establish a base at New Providence. One of the circumstances was naming of a new and lively King to the throne of Spain which led to increased Spanish naval activity. Spanish warships drove out logwood cutters from their traditional working areas in the Gulf of Mexico, and they joined forces with Henry Jennings. Jennings had obtained a privateering commission from Lord Hamilton, Governor of Jamaica, to hunt down pirates. Instead he and some friends sailed over to the

Edward Teach, the pirate Blackbeard who terrorized
the Caribbean

Straits of Florida where Spanish salvage ships were busy raising gold and silver from the wrecks of a Spanish convoy driven ashore in a hurricane in 1714. Jennings and his friends attacked a salvage camp and loaded their ships with loot, adding more to it when they encountered a Spanish vessel. Jennings was the leader, and his suggestion of a pirate stronghold at New Providence was taken up happily. Soon New Providence was the home port for the likes of Edward Teach, known as Blackbeard; Charles Vane; Benjamin Hornigold; Calico Jack Rackham and his mistress, Ann Bonny.

The pirates attacked shipping of all nations, and the British government decided to deal with the problem. It was thought that offering a pardon to the pirates might reduce their number. One Governor who received the information was Benjamin Bennett of Bermuda, who decided to send his son to the Bahamas with the offer. Captain Bennett was seized on arrival, and held until a large number of pirates had gathered. They debated the offer at length, until finally Jennings spoke up in favour of taking it. Young Bennett was released and sent home to tell his father, and a number of pirates followed Jennings to Bermuda. Jennings had Bermudian relations, and no doubt pirate gold helped to establish Jennings, Tucker & Co., a great Bermuda trading firm of the 18th century.

Pirate attacks continued, and Bermuda captains whose ships were looted by pirates brought back word to Bennett that Blackbeard and Major Stede Bonnet planned to attack the island, which would have made an ideal pirate base. Once again the Bermuda militia were put on guard and men kept home to garrison the forts. Blackbeard captured a rich French prize and took it into North Carolina to loot it and forgot about Bermuda. Soon afterwards two Virginia sloops manned by Royal Navy sailors attacked Blackbeard, who died shortly before his fellow pirates surrendered. The sloops sailed back to Virginia with his head swinging beneath the bowsprit of one of them.

By this time the intrepid Governor Woodes Rogers had re-established law in New Providence and the rest of the Bahamas chain.

Bermudian Sailors

The crews of Bermuda ships were composed of both black and white men, and their adventures were by no means confined to salt raking. Governor John Hope has told us what generally went on during the 18th century. The small fast ships would slip out through the Bermuda reefs and head first for the Turks Islands. There the skippers would land their white crews, who would stay in Turks for up to a year, while the captains and the black sailors ventured further south 'a-marooning' as Governor Hope put it. This mean 'fishing for turtle, diving upon wrecks and sometimes trading with pirates'.

If they were lucky in their marooning they sailed to Curacao or St Eustatius or St Thomas or to the French Islands 'where they are always well receiv'd without any questions asked' and sold the cargo – and sometimes the ship too. If the ship was not sold they went back to Turks, picked up the salt cargo and the rest of the crew and went off to North America to sell the salt before coming home to Bermuda. The men had an adventurous time, with the chance that they would come home rich men weighed against the danger of fever or shipwreck and sudden death, but in many ways life was harder for the women. They were left at home, and when the white sails of the ship dipped over the horizon there was no saying when they would see their menfolk again, if ever. It took strength for one parent to bring up families, and that same strength remains with the island today.

There are many tales told about those seafaring times, of which a few are related below.

Thomas Tew's voyage

A number of Bermudians took part in a highly successful piratical voyage. The story starts in 1691 when Thomas Tew, a Rhode Islander, arrived in Bermuda. Tew had some money and, backed by several Bermudians, invested it in the sloop *Amity*. He obtained a letter-of-marque from Governor Isaac Richier and was given the job of capturing a French trading post on the River Gambia in Africa.

Tew sailed from Bermuda in company with another vessel captained by George Dew. Dew's vessel sprung her mast and put back to Bermuda, where he eventually settled and took to the law. He became a Church Warden of St Peter's, and in 1700 the owner of the charming St George's cottage which still exists and is now called 'The Old Rectory'.

The crew of the Amity seizes an Arabian ship (reconstruction) – note that there are both black and white sailors in the crew

Tew carried on. One day he suggested to his crew that he knew a way to make them rich forever. 'A gold chain or a wooden leg! We'll stand by you!' the crew is reported to have said, and Tew headed around the Cape of Good Hope and up the East African coast toward the Red Sea. Their luck was good: they fell in with a large and richly laden Arabian vessel carrying 300 soldiers and much gold. The Bermudians attacked, swarming aboard the larger ship, and her cowardly crew surrendered. Each man's share of the booty was £3000.

The story is told by Captain Charles Johnson, which might be a pen name for the famous English writer Daniel Defoe, author of *Robinson Crusoe*. Johnson says that Tew and his men met Captain Misson, a French pirate, but many knowledgeable persons suspect that Misson is a fictional character. Misson, said Johnson, had created a settlement which he called Libertatia, where there were no slaves and black and white mingled in equality. Tew is said to have joined forces with Misson until Misson died when his ship foundered in a gale. Tew then returned to the Atlantic, leaving a number of his original crew who preferred to live in Madagascar, and bringing other pirates back with him.

Tew landed with £80 000 in booty, and his personal share was said to be £12 000. The Bermudian shareholders in his enterprise sent to Rhode Island for their share and Tew took their emissary to places where he had buried it and dug up enough to make them rich men.

The story of Captain Lewis

Another tale with an unhappy ending tells of the encounter in 1692 of several Bermuda ships with Captain John Lewis, who was a pirate from boyhood. He became a pirate captain when he ran away from Havana with six companions in a canoe, and surprised a small Spanish vessel. Then he captured several more ships and gathered about 40 followers.

From one of the captured ships he learned that a fine Bermuda-built brigantine under the command of a Captain Tucker lay in the Bay of Campeachy in the Gulf of Mexico. Lewis decided to have her, and offered Tucker 10 000 pieces of eight. Tucker refused to sell, and called together the captains of ten other small Bermuda vessels nearby. He suggested that each let him have some men, and he would fight Lewis in an attempt to keep them all safe. The captains refused, but they did agree to set sail immediately.

Then the wind failed, but Lewis came on anyway, using oars. Once more Tucker signalled the other vessels, urging them to send men aboard, but they still refused. The wind sprang up again and Captain Tucker trimmed his sails, let loose a broadside into the pirate ship and escaped. Captain Joseph Dill fired two guns into the pirate, but then one of his cannon burst, killing three men. Other captains tamely surrendered. Lewis went from one ship to another, stealing cargo and money. He either persuaded or forced 40 black sailors and one white carpenter to join him, and took the biggest sloop for his piratical adventures.

It must have been a sad day for Bermuda when the other vessels came back with fortunes gone and loved ones missing. Some of the lost sailors may have made their way home, but the story of Lewis and the captains who succeeded him is evidence that many of them went to Madagascar, which had become a pirate stronghold.

The behaviour of pirates varied. Some would use their piratical reputations to scare merchant skippers into submission and then loot their ships, leaving the ships' company alone, while others delighted in torture, becoming more sadistic with each capture. One such person was Spriggs, a New Englander. When he captured Nicholas Trott's ship he claimed to be angry at finding so little loot and therefore encouraged his men to hoist the sailors up into the rigging, one after another, and then for the fun of it to let go the ropes and watch them bounce on the deck. Those that survived were freed.

Captains Bowen and North

Two Bermudians who became notable pirates were Nathaniel North and John Bowen. North, the son of a sawyer, was a strong swimmer and managed to escape twice from Royal Navy ships after he had been impressed. Eventually he found his way to Madagascar, and after many vicissitudes and adventures joined forces with Bowen, who was a descendant of Richard Norwood.

They took part in the capture of the ship *Speaker* and cruised successfully along the coast of India. Then, heading back to Madagascar, on 7 January 1702, the ship suddenly crashed into a reef off the coast of Mauritius. Most of the crew reached shore, and hired a vessel from the Dutch and returned to Madagascar. There they captured a Scottish ship called the *Speedy Return*. After another successful raid on the coast of India they changed ships. On the way back to Madagascar Captain Bowen decided to stay ashore in the Mascarene Islands, but his time was short. Six months later he died, and was buried under a road, as the priest refused him a place in the cemetery because he was a heretic.

North had many other adventures before he settled in Madagascar at Ambonavoula. He dominated local affairs and developed enemies, who one night murdered him in his bed. His friends avenged his death in a bloody war which continued for seven years.

The treasure reef

When Bermudians went 'a-marooning' as Governor Hope put it, they were always hopeful that they might be able to follow the great find of William Phipps. Phipps heard about a Spanish treasure ship, the *Nuestra Senora de la Concepcion* which had been shipwrecked on a reef north of Hispaniola which came to be called the Ambrosias Reef. King Charles II was interested in the treasure and allowed Phipps to use a royal vessel, the *Rose*, for the search. The voyage was a failure, and it was on his way back to England that he put into Bermuda and helped save Coney before Sharpe arrived.

The King had had enough of treasure hunting – except for the percentage which was reserved for the crown – but a nobleman, the Duke of Albemarle, was prepared to back a second voyage. The Duke sent out two ships with Captain Phipps in command. Divers kept searching sections of the reef without success, and it looked as if the second expedition would be another failure. Phipps took the larger vessel, the *James and Mary*, to Hispaniola to trade and buy provisions, and while he was gone the men aboard the *Henry* found the wreck. One story has it that an Indian diver was asked to bring up a pretty piece of coral which could be seen from the boat. When he came back to the surface he reported seeing a number of cannon. More diving brought up the first pieces of treasure, but bad weather forced Captain Francis Rogers to sail away from the dangerous reef, and so he sought out Phipps to give him the good news. The two vessels returned, but there were only four divers and for several days progress was slow. Then came an alarm: two vessels were seen sailing towards them.

It turned out that they were a Bermudian under the command of William Davis and a Jamaican under Abraham Adderley. Phipps did the sensible thing – he hired the vessels and their crews to speed up the diving. The Bermudian had a diving bell, which briefly turned out to be a very successful aid, until a storm came up. The problem was that the mother vessel had to anchor close to the wreck's position, and the storm put her in jeopardy of the same reefs that had caused the *Almiranta* shipwreck.

Finally, with supplies running low and perhaps one third of the treasure salvaged, it was time for Phipps' squadron to return to England with nearly 70 000 lbs of silver. Adderley and Davis were sworn to secrecy, but a few months later, when Phipps brought another fleet of five ships from England to continue diving, 32 colonial vessels were there working away as fast as they could. As soon as the new squadron came in sight several vessels hauled their anchors and set sail. The newcomers had pretty well cleared the more accessible parts of the wreck, and therefore the expedition was a failure. The next known successful expedition took place in 1978, when the wreck was found again by the Seaquest Company led by Burt Webber. They managed to overcome the difficult problem of digging through the overgrowth of coral to reach the rest of the wreck.

In Bermuda the returning treasure hunters found that the Governor was demanding a tenth of their find for the King. Over £5000 was secured, but when the King's representatives arrived during a trip to most of the colonies and pointed out that the King was due one half, very little more was forthcoming. Bermudians, a disappointed official claimed, had a saying that a man could never get an estate by being honest.

The Bermuda Rig

It was about this time that the Bermuda sail came into sufficient prominence to be recognised as a special rig. A triangular sail, in those days it was loose-footed without a boom. Bermudians found that it was excellent in making a sailboat work its way against the wind, but only since the First World War has it been accepted by yachtsmen as the best sail for dinghies and yachts.

The rig is similar to a Dutch rig of the time and may have been introduced to Bermuda by a Dutch shipwright who was saved from a shipwreck and took employment here under Governor Nathaniel Butler. Bermudians used the rig for three centuries before it received worldwide recognition. Its final home-grown form is the rig still used in Bermuda sailing dinghies.

The Militia

During most of Bermuda's history Bermudians have taken some of the responsibility for the island's defence. Governor Moore and the first settlers manned the cannon at Castle Island and drove off the Spaniards. In a different role the Militia became 'the Army', proclaimed allegiance to King Charles II and made John Trimingham Governor, which shows their power at that time.

Some of the small militia forts can still be seen. There is one near the Martello Tower at Ferry Reach, and another at the east end of Church Bay. Gates Fort, St George's, (more properly Town Cut Battery according to Dr Edward Harris) is a reconstruction of an important militia fort and battery. Across from Castle Harbour

*A Bermuda trading sloop, part of a crude picture of
St George's waterfront, probably made by a sailor*

is Southampton Fort on Southampton Island, still almost exactly as it was built by Governor Butler.

Records show that the militia included both black and white men, even when most black men were slaves. During Governor Bennett's time 600 slaves were provided with lances and drilled with white musketeers, but on several occasions during the same administration the number of white sailors on outward-bound Bermuda vessels was reduced to keep more white men on the island.

The militia tended to fade away in times of peace during the 18th century, but would be whipped into shape again when war threatened. They were also called on when a slave rising seemed possible in 1761. During the 19th century the militia disappeared. It was finally revived in a different form when the Bermuda Militia Artillery and the Bermuda Volunteer Rifle Corps were formed in the 1890s. The units underwent various changes, finally amalgamating and becoming the Bermuda Regiment in the 1960s.

Jokes were often made about the militia of the 18th century, but without them and the cannon they manned Bermuda would have seemed an easy prey to pirates or enemy warships. Bermuda's amateur soldiers played an important role in keeping Bermuda under one flag throughout her history.

SOURCES
Earle, *The Wreck of the Almiranta*.
Harris, *Bermuda Forts*.
Johnson, *A General History of the Robberies and Murders of the Most Notorious Pirates*.
Newman, *Company of Adventurers*, Vol. I.
Zuill, W.S., *The Pirate Menace*.

10

Slavery in Bermuda and the mid-18th Century

Slavery in Bermuda

Slavery in Bermuda may have had more in common with the slavery which used to exist in West Africa, where many slaves learned trades or were domestic servants, than with the pattern of plantation slavery which existed in the West Indies and America. In the West Indies and in the southern colonies of the American coast there were large cotton and sugar plantations on which most of the work was done by slaves. In Bermuda there were no such plantations, and while slaves were expected to till the soil from time to time, there were no large groups of men, women and children gathered under the control of one estate.

In the case of Bermuda it is difficult to work out exactly how slaves and free people lived together and how slaves were treated. We do know that the ownership of slaves was spread widely among the white people, and that the slaves themselves either did household work, mason's and carpenter's work, farm work, shipbuilding, or were sent to sea in Bermuda's merchant fleet. The fact that Bermuda ships were partly manned by slaves was vitally important for the island's economy, for the Bermuda shipowners, using this cheaper labour, were able to underbid competitors for cargoes. They were also helped by other factors such as the excellence of the design of their ships and the strength and endurance of the cedar wood.

It appears that few slaves came directly to Bermuda from Africa. Some Bermuda ships carried slaves from Africa to the West Indian or American markets, but most slaves coming to Bermuda had already been taken from Africa and landed somewhere else on the Western side of the Atlantic. Occasionally they had been working for masters in Britain. In any case, not all Bermuda slaves were Africans. There were also a number of Indians, both from the North American coast and from the West Indies.

The *Edwin* brought the first recorded Indian and the first black man to Bermuda in 1616, and other black people were brought in, some from England, partly as agricultural experts, before the first major importations in 1619. The ship they came on was perhaps a pirate vessel; in any case the slaves were given to the Governor, Miles Kendall, as a present. Later when Nathaniel Butler arrived and Kendall went to England, Butler seized the slaves for the Bermuda Company and assigned them to his great friend, the Earl of Warwick. Thereafter there was considerable dispute as to who the rightful owner was.

White slaves were imported as a result of Cromwell's victories over the Irish, as were indentured servants, who were bound to work a set number of years to pay off their passage money and were sometimes treated worse than slaves: a cruel boss would want to get as much as possible out of an indentured servant during the seven years limit of his investment.

Thirty-six Indian slaves were brought in in 1644, when Captain William Jackson arrived with his fleet after a successful sweep through the Caribbean against the Spanish colonists. Most of them were women. It was a large group to become part of a small population. Most of the island's slaves were imported in the early days of Bermuda's history, and by 1670 the Government was trying to stop people bringing in any more, because large numbers of slaves were not necessary on a small island. By 1699 the population consisted of 3615 white people and 2247 black people. The figures included 803 white men and 566 black and 1050 white women and 649 black, as well as children.

This meant that early on the Bermuda people started to develop special qualities, responding to the island, the sea, the climate and special economic conditions. The races became mixed, though not completely, so that now the Bermuda people have a wide variety of skin colours, ranging from blue-black to pink-white. Despite skin colour differences the fact of living together for nearly 400 years makes us, black and white, one people with a shared culture.

Attempts at rebellion

Not all Indians and Africans in Bermuda were slaves, judging by the early records. In 1656, for instance, all free black people were ordered to go to Eleuthera in the Bahamas. This was because there had been a plot 'that the Negroes in this island had contrived for cutting off and destroying the English in the night', according to the old records. Four slaves and one free man, Willi fforce, were alleged to be the conspirators, but the evidence cannot have been strong because only two, named in the records as Black Tom and Cabilecto, were ordered to be executed. However a proclamation was issued preventing all black people from stirring at night from their owners' houses unless they had a pass, stopping black people from engaging in trade and banishing all free Negroes to Eleuthera, including Willi fforce.

This appears to be the second time white settlers feared a slave uprising. The first time was around 1629. The third occurred in 1673. On Christmas Eve of that year the Governor, Sir John Heydon, and his Council found six black men guilty of playing a major role in the plot. No executions were ordered, but the six men were ordered to have their noses slit, to be branded with the letter 'R' on the forehead and to be whipped. Other slaves were also ordered to be branded and shipped. The punishments were carried out at 'ye bottom of ye Laine' which may be the present Foot-of-the-Lane. As well as punishing the ringleaders, once again orders were issued restricting all black people.

Apparently there were no further troubles between black and white until 1750. At that time the garrison of the regular British Army, the Independent Company of Foot, had been sent to the Bahamas where pirates were running rampant again. This time a few slaves planned to poison their masters. It ended in the famous execution of Sarah Bassett, who was accused of attempting to poison her master and mistress and a fellow slave, and who was regarded as the ringleader. It is said that she was executed near a well which once stood close to Point Finger Road, Paget. She was brought from St George's for the execution and on the way a number of people passed. 'Don't hurry,' she told them, 'the fun doesn't start until I get there.' It was a very hot day, and ever since a hot day has been called a Sarah Bassett day.

The attempted revolt in 1761 seems to have caused more fear among the white people than any of the previous ones. We cannot be certain of the precise causes, apart from general discontent among the slaves, but there was a series of events which built up tension. Early in the year a black man who raped a white woman was tried and ordered to be executed on 24 June at Gibbons Island, Smith's, and his body was hung in chains between 9 a.m. and noon. Later in the same year a free black woman, Rachel Fubler, complained that Edward Seymour had taken two of her children. The matter was placed in the hands of the Attorney General, who was ordered to take steps to free them. The records do not clearly indicate the outcome of this.

There were several cases of poisoning in the island which reminded people of the plot of 1730. The climax came on 12 October 1761. John Vickers of Smith's Parish overheard rebellious talk among a group of slaves, in particular three named as Nat, George and Peter. George was reported to have said that there would be a great victory gained soon, or if not one-half to two-thirds of the Negroes in Bermuda would be hanged. White people realized that this time the plot was widespread, and white fears led to the banning of the 5 November Guy Fawkes celebration with its gunpowder fireworks. The outcome of the attempted revolt was the execution of six people and the revival of many harsh laws against free and slave black people.

The fact that there were attempted slave revolts shows that a number of black people had strong grievances about their treatment in Bermuda, but the fact that none of them actually roused the country to civil war, as happened elsewhere, may show that many black people did not find their position so intolerable that they were willing to take the risks involved in a full-scale uprising.

An indication of this is the way seventy slaves on a Bermuda privateer, the *Regulator*, behaved when they had a chance to escape from the island. During the American Revolutionary War the *Regulator* was captured by American ships and sent into Boston. The crew were given the chance of staying in Boston or being exchanged for captured Americans. They elected to be exchanged and were placed in a cartel to sail to New York, then held by the British forces. Once at sea the Bermudians forced the captain of the cartel vessel to change course and take them to home to Bermuda.

The relationship between master and slave

Masters and slaves were often dependent on each other, and there are many tales which indicate mutual affection. A situation which must have occurred many times in seafaring Bermuda is recorded in the case of a widow, Mrs Forbes, who was mostly dependent on the earnings of her slave, Mingo.

Some owners recompensed their slaves' faithful service by setting them free in their wills; Governor John Hope so appreciated the way in which a slave named Nancy looked after his wife when she was ill that he purchased her and set her free. Because of actions similar to this there were about 100 freed slaves in Bermuda by the end of the 18th century.

The sale of slaves appears to have been rare, and the procedure was difficult. A New Englander reported that the sale of a slave in Bermuda was as reproachful as the sale of a son elsewhere. The children of slaves became slaves, which created legal problems when slaves belonging to two different masters married. It was agreed in the 17th century that the first child would go to the owner of the wife, the second to the owner of the husband, and so on.

A story is told of a young man named John who belonged to a family living in Flatts who disapproved of his visits to his girl friend, who was owned by another family living on the other side of Harrington Sound. Slaves walking along the roads at night were liable to get into trouble, so John used to swim to see his beloved. His owner discovered this, and bound John to a stake with a chain. One night John, still determined to see his girl, found he could not wriggle out of his fetters, so he pulled up the stake and swam once more to see his sweetheart. This softened the owners' hearts and they allowed the couple to marry. They probably jumped over a broomstick together several times, which was the custom in Bermuda as well as in parts of America. Although the story has a happy ending it also tells a great deal about the power of masters over slaves, and the shackling indicates what slaves could be made to endure.

White Christians varied in their attitudes towards slaves. In the early days of Bermuda most preachers felt that slaves should be christened and taught about Christianity, but there were slave owners who felt that Christianity only made the slaves restless. Theologians battled about the question, but by the mid-18th century, in Bermuda anyway, most slaves appear to have been expected to go to church, but were expected to sit in galleries. Punishment for slaves was often a flogging, which might well be administered by a parish official who became known as the 'Jumper' because he made people jump.

Bermuda in the mid-18th Century

The Bermuda of that time appears to have been a relatively simple, poor community. People lived off fish a good deal – salt cod with potatoes and bananas is still a traditional Sunday breakfast – and imported flour to make bread. They grew or imported corn (maize). Another local food which has continued in use to the present day was cassava (from the root of the manioc bush which is also the source of tapioca). This provided a flour from a locally grown crop. Nowadays Cassava pie remains a favourite Bermuda Christmas dish. It is similar to English meat pies such as the Cornish pasty in that the highly spiced dough not only forms the crust but is also mixed with the meat filling of beef, chicken and pork.

Transportation from one place to another was normally by boat. There were probably few horses, and the old roads such as the tribe roads (a few of which still exist in what seems to be their early form) look as if they were just wide enough to allow a barrel to be rolled along. Flour may well have been transported in this way.

Freemasonry in Bermuda traces back to this era. Both William Popple, Governor at this time, and his brother and predecessor, Alured Popple, were Masons, and William Popple succeeded in establishing the first lodge in 1761. Apparently the lodge faded out of existence, but Masonry was re-established before the end of the century and has endured ever since. The first lodges were white, but, looking ahead into the next century, the first integrated lodge, Hannibal No. 224, was established in 1867.

The Bermudian

When Nathaniel Tucker was sent to the North Carolina in the early 1770s to further his education he became extremely homesick for his native island, and wrote a poem, based on Oliver Goldsmith's 'The Deserted Village', called *The Bermudian*. Reading between the lines of this charming work tells us something of life in the island. The following lines tell about the fisherman and his family:

> Before Aurora gilds the Eastern skies
> The sun-burnt tenants of the cottage rise;
> With many a yawn their drowsy comrades hail,
> Rub their dim eyes, and taste the morning gale.
> Some bear the basket, plenteously supply'd
> With hooks and lines, the able fisher's pride;
> Others with dexterous hands and toils display
> Well skilled to circumvent the scaly prey;
> With wide-extended nets the shores they sweep,
> Or man the bark, and plough the finny deep.
> The little urchins, playing on the strand,
> At distance kens the bark returned to land;
> Meanwhile the housewife decks the cleanly board,
> With all her homely cottage can afford;
> Her little brood are seated to their wish;
> And taste the blessing of the smoking dish;
> Of childish stories prattle all the while,
> Regarding either parent with a finny smile;
> The finny monster's grateful taste admire,
> And for it bless their providential sire.
> He with delight the youthful tribe surveys,
> His gladden'd eyes still brighten as they gaze;
> Of earthly joys he knows no higher pitch,
> And bids the prince be great, the miser rich.

SOURCES
Ives, *The Rich Papers, Letters from Bermuda*.
Lefroy, *Memorials of the Bermudas* (3rd edition).
Packwood, *Chained on the Rock – Slavery in Bermuda*.
Smith, *Slavery in Bermuda*.
Tucker, *The Bermudian*.
Wilkinson, *The Adventurers of Bermuda* (2nd edition).
Wilkinson, *Bermuda in the Old Empire*.

11

Gunpowder, Revolution and Forts

The Gunpowder Steal

On the evening of 14 August 1775 a group of men came ashore
from some whaleboats at Tobacco Bay, St George's. They crept up
the short steep hill to where the colony's gunpowder magazine lay.
Some kept watch. Others climbed to the roof and broke off some
slates, crept in through the hole, jumped down and forced open the
door. Soon the small barrels of gunpowder were being rolled down
to the bay.

The lookouts were suddenly frightened when a man in uniform
approached through the night. Taking no chances, they struck him
down and buried him in the Governor's garden. His bones, so oral
history says, were found 100 years later when the foundations were
being dug for a replacement for old St Peter's Church (a replacement
which was never completed and is now known as 'the Unfinished
Church'). Some fragments of a French uniform and buttons were
found, which is thought to explain why a French officer on parole in
St George's disappeared that hot summer's night.

The gunpowder was taken by the whaleboats to two American
ships, the *Lady Catherine* of Virginia and the *Charleston and
Savannah Pacquet* of South Carolina. It was being taken to an
America at war, a war against Great Britain which was to reshape
the destiny of the western Atlantic and the world. The 13 American
colonies had rebelled because of harsh British retaliation after a
Boston mob had thrown tea overboard from British ships in Boston
Harbour.

The Gunpowder Steal, 1775 (reconstruction)

Colonel Henry Tucker: portrait on display at the
President Henry Tucker House

It is thought that roughly one-third of the American colonists were willing revolutionaries, one-third were active loyalists, and one-third would have preferred not to be involved on either side. Perhaps the same was true for Bermuda at that time: certainly the raid on the magazine was carried out with Bermudian help. Even now, however, the details are not known, which is not surprising since the plot almost certainly involved members of several prominent families, in particular the Tuckers, who could have lost their lives if their parts had been discovered.

They stole the powder because the newly formed American Continental Congress had stopped the export of food supplies to all

British colonies. A group of prominent Bermudians, led by Colonel Henry Tucker, went to plead Bermuda's cause with the Congress, since the import of food was essential to the existence of the island, and offered to bring salt to America. The Congress, not realising how important salt would soon become, turned the Bermudians down, but said they might change their minds in return for gunpowder.

Was self-interest mixed with this plea for food for Bermuda? Some scholars believe that the Tuckers were primarily interested in maintaining their trading contacts and connections. Could Britain have supplied food? Perhaps, but the British were forced to send food to their armed forces in America, and were even asked to send fodder for the Army's horses. Feeding Bermuda would have been an additional strain on stretched British resources.

General George Washington himself wrote to the Bermudians about gunpowder. The letter was never presented to Bermudians as the ship carrying Washington's emissary arrived after the powder was stolen, but it is important for it shows how great the need was. Nicely calculated to arouse the feelings of fellow colonists, it was composed before the Continental Congress passed the Declaration of Independence.

Gentlemen,

In the great conflict which agitates this continent, I cannot doubt but the asserters of freedom and the right of the constitution are possessed of your most favourable regards and wishes for success. As descendants of free men, and heirs with us of the same glorious inheritance, we flatter ourselves that, though divided by our situation, we are firmly united in sentiment. The cause of virtue and liberty is confined to no continent or climate. It comprehends, within its capacious limits, the wise and good, however dispersed and separated in space and distance.

You need not be informed that the violence and rapacity of a tyrannic ministry have forced the citizens of America, your brother colonists, into arms. We equally detest and lament the prevalence of those counsels which have led to the effusion of so much human blood, and left us no alternative but a civil war, or a base submission.

The wise disposer of all events has hitherto smiled upon our virtuous efforts. Those mercenary troops, a few of whom lately boasted of subjugating this vast continent, have been checked in their earliest ravages, and are now actually encircled in a small space, their arms disgraced, and suffering all the calamities of a siege.

The virtue, spirit and union of the provinces leave them nothing to fear, but the want of ammunition. The application

George Washington

of our enemies to foreign states, and their vigilance upon our coasts, are the only efforts they have made against us with success. Under these circumstances, and with these sentiments, we have turned our eyes to you, Gentlemen, for relief.

We are informed that there is a very large magazine on your island under a very feeble guard. We would not wish to involve you in an opposition in which, from your situation, we should be unable to support you; we know not, therefore, to what extent to solicit your assistance in availing ourselves of this supply; but if your favour and friendship to North America and its liberties have not been misrepresented, I persuade myself you may, consistent with your own safety, promote and further the scheme, so as to give it the fairest prospect of success.

Be assured that in this case the whole power and exertion of my influence will be made with the honourable Continental Congress, that your island may not only be supplied with provisions, but experience every other mark of affection and friendship which the grateful citizens of a free country can bestow on its brethren and benefactors.

George Washington

After the Powder Was Stolen ...

On the morning of 15 August Governor George James Bruere found out about the theft. He immediately issued a proclamation:

POWDER STEAL

Save your country from ruin, which may hereafter happen. The Powder stole out of the magazine late last night cannot be carried far as the wind is light.

A GREAT REWARD

will be given to any person that can make a proper discovery before the magistrates.

Not only was the unhappy Governor's advertisement a failure – he then had great difficulty in sending word to General Gage, commanding the British troops in Boston, to tell him what had happened. No Bermuda ships wanted to sail, and when Bruere found a messenger an attempt was made to steal the letter. However, the message did eventually get through. Bruere must have felt that he was almost alone in an island filled with revolutionaries, and his troubles with the House of Assembly would have made him feel even more isolated. However, it seems likely that many citizens were in fact loyal, even if they were cautious about expressing their feelings.

Bruere had a year to endure before Royal Navy ships arrived, but when they came they strained loyalties. In an attempt to stop trade with the American colonies they captured Bermuda ships, burnt one Bermuda vessel in Ely's Harbour, and sent landing forces into warehouses where they thought contraband was hidden.

The Morgans' Attack

On 14 June 1777, two American privateers commanded by members of the Morgan family of Southampton put into the West End. A small British battery manned by sailors from HMS *Nautilus*, at anchor in Castle Harbour, was quickly abandoned and the 'tars' fled back to their ship. For six days the *Nautilus* never stirred while the privateers spiked the guns of the battery and had a free run, filling their water barrels and obtaining some privately held guns. No one called out the militia, and Governor Bruere clung to St George's.

Some say the cloud which forms over Bermuda on hot summer days is called Morgans' Cloud because it is symbolic of the dark moment when Bermudians attacked Bermuda.

Loyalist Privateers

In 1778 France declared war on Britain and in the autumn British troops arrived to protect Bermuda against possible French attack. American privateers, loyal to Britain, used Bermuda as a base. Most of them were owned by a Virginian family named Goodrich, and at one point several of the Goodrich vessels controlled Chesapeake Bay. Bermudians did not like these vessels because they captured Bermuda ships as well as American.

The loyalist privateers were such a nuisance to the Continental Congress that they decided to try and capture Bermuda. Four warships were sent and arrived off the island on 1 December 1779 – a few hours too late. That morning a British convoy had put in with reinforcements for the garrison, and the chance the Americans had of capturing Bermuda disappeared. This was the only plan for capturing Bermuda which came close to success, but the Americans kept their eye on the island, and devised several schemes for capturing the colony.

Soon afterwards Bermuda was hit by a terrible epidemic. It started in prison (the building is now the St George's Post Office) among American prisoners of war, and quickly spread throughout Bermuda. Resistance to disease was low because of the great shortage of food, and the population was decimated.

The following year, in September, Bruere died after enduring one of the most difficult administrations that a loyal Governor ever had to undergo. He was succeeded by his son, another George, who quickly proved himself equally loyal but more energetic and able than his father. Any lingering thoughts Bermudians might have had about joining the United States were squashed, although by now it was becoming apparent that Britain was losing the war. France and Spain had joined the United States, and in October 1781 the combined American and French forces won the twin victories of The Battle of the Capes (a sea battle) and Yorktown (a siege), resulting in the capture of Lord Cornwallis's Army. Peace was signed in 1783 when Britain recognized US independence.

Gibraltar of the West

With the ending of the war it was clear that Britain's position in the Western Atlantic had completely changed. The great chain of ports and cities which had been available to her forces up and down the American coast were gone. Instead, they were left with Halifax in the north in Canada, Bermuda in the middle and the Bahamas in the south.

In Bermuda the younger Governor Bruere was succeeded by William Browne, a loyalist from New England. Under his leadership Bermuda petitioned London to become 'the Gibraltar of the West'. Nothing happened immediately, but throughout the next century the fortifications of Bermuda were constantly improved, and Bermuda moved from being a seafaring community dependent on her ships and salt trade to being a fortress island.

Work on the 'Gibraltar of the West' began just after the outbreak of war between Britain and France. France had executed its King, Royal Family and many of its nobles as well as numerous innocent persons who were simply denounced to the revolutionary authorities. Britain held aloof from efforts by other countries to put down the revolution, but in February 1793, France declared war. It was a war which, with a brief recess, was to rage until 1814, breaking out again briefly in 1815.

By June, 1793, the first formal moves to improve Bermuda's fortifications were started. Captain Andrew Durnford, an Army engineer, outlined to the House of Assembly the military needs for the defence of the island. He wanted four parcels of land in St George's and one in Southampton.

The following year Captain Hurd of the Royal Navy, who had been surveying Bermuda waters for some time, discovered that quite large vessels could sail from Five Fathom Hole around St Catherine's Point and up to the West End of the island. Captain Hurd was under the orders of Vice-Admiral Sir George Murray and the big area of deep water inside the reefs north of St George's was named Murray's Anchorage in his honour, a name it retains today.

Admiral Murray's flagship, the 74-gun line-of-battle ship *Resolution*, was successfully piloted into the anchorage in April, 1795, by Pilot Jemmy Darrell, a Bermuda slave. The Admiral was so pleased with his work that he asked the Governor and Council to give him his freedom, which was done.

The Admiralty decided in 1795 that they wanted to build a dockyard at Ireland Island and a depot in St George's, but there was to be a delay of 15 years before the work at the West End started.

Bermuda Privateers

Britain was facing enormous problems at the time. From 1793 onwards the French won a series of victories on land and threatened British seapower. One of the threats came through the commissioning of privateers, which swarmed the Atlantic. Bermuda vessels were captured by these ships, but Bermudians also took out letters-of-marque and preyed on French shipping and property. Particular targets were Frenchmen escaping from Haiti with their families and house- hold goods as a slave revolt became more and more successful. (The revolt started in 1794 and was led by Toussaint L'Ouverture, Jean- Jacques Dessalines and Henri Christophe. It finally succeeded in 1804).

Among the Bermudians who skippered privateers was Hezekiah Frith, who made a series of successful voyages using mixed slave and free crews. The slaves were entered in the ship's books for a share in the profits, although some or all of this money must have gone to their owners. Slaves were hired out for crew as they were for other jobs.

One of Frith's voyages ended in disaster. In 1797 his vessel, the *Hezekiah*, was taken by the Spanish frigate *Juno*. There were 56 slaves aboard the privateer, and all were considered lawful prizes by the Spanish, although Frith attempted to offer himself as ransom for them. He was soon freed, and returned to Bermuda to build a new ship and go to sea many more times.

One of the captured slaves, John Graisberry, finally succeeded in returning to Bermuda in 1844, nearly 50 years afterwards. He said that all but three of the crew had died in that time, and attrib- uted his own long life to drinking rum only and that seldom, and never becoming intoxicated. He had endured 22 years of slavery in Cuba, had been released, and finally been given a passage to Bermuda by the British Consul.

Renewed Trouble in the Atlantic

As the new century dawned the international situation was chang- ing. In the 1790s the Americans, annoyed at British and French attacks on their ships, armed their vessels and sent their navy to sea in an undeclared war principally against the French. France, however, had a great prize to offer America, and in 1803 President Thomas Jefferson made a deal to buy the whole of the enormous but unsettled part of middle America then owned by France and known as the Louisiana territory.

The great Louisiana purchase seems to have inflamed a number of Americans with a desire for even more land. Britain, the old enemy, was busy fighting France, so British Canada looked almost defenceless. In addition, as part of a campaign to stop countries not involved in the war from trading with France, the Royal Navy was snatching American merchantmen, drafting into the British service members of their crews and sending the ships into British ports for long drawn-out legal proceedings.

Tom Moore

One of the ports was Bermuda, and the Court of Vice-Admiralty became busy. Among other tasks Courts of Vice-Admiralty decided whether a ship captured by a Royal Navy vessel or a privateer was a legitimate prize of war. Officers of the Court were appointed in London, and thus it was that friends of the impoverished Irish poet Tom Moore persuaded the government to appoint him to the sinecure post of Registrar of the Court of Vice-Admiralty in Bermuda.

The bust of the Irish poet Tom Moore decorates a small garden near the King's Square, St George's

Tom only stayed in Bermuda a few months, but he was remembered for his London wit and his popularity with young women. Soon he found a deputy to carry out his duties and returned to London. The post continued in the hands of the deputy for many years, until one day in 1818 the deputy absconded with £6 000 in the keeping of the court. Moore had to run away to France for a while until the debt could be compromised and settled.

Tom's real reputation in Bermuda was acquired after he left, when the *Odes to Nea* were published. Nea was the nickname of Hester, the wife of Mr. William Tucker, who had been seen with Tom quite frequently although she was pregnant. So when verses like

> Oh! trust me, 'twas a place, an hour,
> The worst that e'er temptation's power
> Could tangle me or you in!
> Sweet Nea! Let us roam no more
> Along that wild and lonely shore
> Such walks will be our ruin!

were published, it naturally caused a good deal of talk!

Tom Moore's restaurant in Hamilton Parish is named after the poet. He did not actually own the building or live in it, but he did visit it a number of times, and one of his poems refers to a calabash tree nearby.

That lay in the future. The immediate reality was that the United States became increasingly annoyed, and the impressment of seamen and the legal delays provided a good excuse for starting hostilities. On 18 June 1812, the US Congress declared war on Britain.

SOURCES

Bowler, *Logistics and the Failure of the British Army in America 1775–1783*.

Wilkinson, *Bermuda in the Old Empire*.

Zuill, W.E.S., *Tom Moore's Bermuda Poems*.

12

The War of 1812

With the start of the war of 1812 Bermuda became a great centre of activity as the hard-pressed Royal Navy stretched the line of its ships still further and started a blockade of the American coast. At first the Navy underestimated the fighting ability of the American sailors and their big frigates, and a number of British ships were defeated in single-ship actions. Only once was the score reversed when HMS *Shannon* defeated USS *Chesapeake* off Boston. The Royal Navy quickly learned to sail their ships only in squadrons, preferably with a heavyweight ship of the line in each one, and eventually, despite the American successes, a large number of American merchantmen and warships were held in port or captured on the high seas.

The successful blockade of the American coast in all seasons from one naval base, Halifax, a depot in Bermuda and auxiliary stations in the Bahamas and West Indies, was a major feat of arms scarcely recognized today by the three nations primarily involved – Britain, Canada and the United States. Bermuda played a fundamental role in the blockade, despite a fearful explosion and a ferocious hurricane.

The explosion occurred on 1 November 1812. An eyewitness at the barracks in St George's described the view across the harbour to Hen Island, where there was a major powder magazine. There was bright sunshine and a placid sky but in the west a black cloud appeared. Soon the scene was changed, as the heavens thundered and lightning flashed.

The electric fluid poured from every quarter of the heavens. It absolutely rained fire. A vivid zig-zag stream of light now darted obliquely toward the harbour – a report as a salvo of a thousand of the heaviest cannon resounded around the vaulted roof of Heaven with appalling reverberations, in the midst of which, and before the preceding flash had vanished, a bright ribbon of flame appeared, encircling the Heavens with terrific brightness, as if the hand of Jove were whirling the bolt around his head, that he might direct his vengeance with unerring aim. Then a vertical stream of fire, more intensely brilliant and appalling than the last, resembling the combustion of a bar of steel in oxygen gas, was seen to dart its prong into the rock where stood the magazine. Simultaneously, therefrom a preter-natural sheet of fire, shooting rubied radiations all around, while one astounding echoless report, such as few ears ever heard, burst forth, making the very island tremble, silencing the wind and absorbing the thunder itself ... it almost seemed as if a raging fire bursting from the centre of the earth, had suddenly reclaimed the islands, originally torn from its bosom, and we were now entombed within its bowels. When sight was restored I looked and behold! the magazine had vanished. Brimstone and fire were raining on the spot; 93 000 leaden balls and 300 shrapnel shells were falling into the dark, sur-rounding water, forming a halo of foam about the rock.[1]

Remarkably, the gunner in charge of the magazine, his wife and family, escaped absolutely unscathed although their cottage was ripped apart.

The hurricane swept across the island on the night of 4 August 1813. Many prizes were anchored in St George's Harbour, and there were fearful scenes as first one vessel and then another dragged their anchors, smashed into other ships, causing them to drag in turn, until in the morning 30 vessels were piled up at the western end of the harbour in Mullet Bay.

The war situation changed enormously in the spring of 1814 when Napolen, Emperor of the French, was defeated and sent to exile on the Mediterranean island of Elba. Veteran units of the highly successful British army, which had been fighting French troops in Spain and France, were detached for service in North America, and ships and troops from several different ports assem-bled at Bermuda.

By July everything was ready, but the ships anchored inside the reef barrier at Murray's Anchorage could not get out because an east wind was blowing. A Bermudian, Joseph Nicholas Hayward, offered to pilot the ships out by a little-known channel near North Rock. The Admiral agreed and the ships set sail.

Sir Harry Smith, an army officer on the big 80-gun flagship HMS *Tonnant*, tells what happened next.

> The passage is most intricate and the pilot directed the helmsman by looking into the water at each of the rocks. It was the most extraordinary thing ever seen, the rocks visible under water all around the ships.
>
> Our pilot, a gentleman, said there was only one part of the passage that gave him any apprehension; there was a turn in it and he feared that the *Tonnant* was so long that her bows would touch; on my honour, when her rudder was clear there was a foot to spare. The breeze was very light and for half an hour it almost died away. The only expression the Admiral was heard to make was: 'Well, if the breeze fails it will be a good turn I have done the Yankees'.[2]

The breeze did not fail, and the ships and the soldiers they carried went on to help with the successful attack on Washington which resulted in the burning of the White House and the Capitol. They followed this up with an attack on Baltimore, which failed thanks in part to the stubborn defence of Fort McHenry – a defence forever remembered in the words of the *Star Spangled Banner*. Another British attack did better, and British ships threaded their way up the Potomac River to the town of Alexandria. American merchant ships sheltering there were sunk, but the British made the townsfolk raise them by threatening to bombard the town. The ships were raised and the squadron and its prizes made their way down the river despite being battered by cannon dragged along the river.

Midshipman Richard Sutherland Dale

The most important prize brought into Bermuda during the war was the big American frigate USS *President*. She was captured in January, 1815, when, under the command of Captain Stephen

Decatur, she put to sea from New York after a gale blew the British blockading squadron offshore. Captain Hayes, in charge of the British squadron, guessed what had happened, worked out Decatur's likely course up the shore of Long Island, and sailed to intercept him. Hayes was successful, and soon the British squadron, consisting of the frigates *Endymion, Pomone* and *Tenedos* and the small ship of the line *Majestic*, sighted the American ship. Probably the *President* could have defeated any one of the frigates on their own, but the presence of the entire squadron forced Decatur to run. HMS *Endymion* gradually caught up with the *President* and yawed time and again, each change of course enabling her to pour broadsides into the *President*'s stern.

Eventually Decatur turned and fought the *Endymion*, but it took two hours before he succeeded in disabling her sufficiently to start running again. But now the *Pomone* and *Tenedos* had come up and Decatur decided he had no chance to escape, so he surrendered. The *President* was brought into St George's as a prize, and a wounded Midshipman, Richard Sutherland Dale, was landed with other American prisoners. A sad tombstone in St Peter's Churchyard, St George's, tells of the kind care St Georgians gave him, and of his death; from time to time a memorial service is held in the graveyard, for he, the first US serviceman memorialized in Bermuda, represents all the US servicemen who have died here.

The sea battle was, in fact, in vain, for peace had been signed between Britain and the United States on Christmas Eve, 1814, before Decatur put to sea. But the treaty was signed in Europe and it was many weeks before HMS *Favourite* could succeed in fighting fierce Atlantic gales to bring the news to this side of the Atlantic.

Duke Of Wellington's Plan

After the war little progress was made on the Bermuda fortifications, but in 1826 the Duke of Wellington devised a scheme for the defence of Bermuda, and his plan was the basis of military plans for over a hundred years. The Duke felt the most important military objective in Bermuda was the dockyard at Ireland Island. He proposed that it be fortified, and Boaz Island as well. Next he turned his attention to the channels through which ships might get inside the reefs. He suggested that the St George's shoreline should be heavily fortified, particularly Fort Catherine, and that the entrance to Castle Harbour should be blocked by sinking a ship there. This part of the plan was never carried out.

Finally he worried about the possibility that ships might come in close to the South Shore reefs and send soldiers ashore in boats onto the beaches. To deal with this problem he proposed that a reserve of 400 men with a brigade of artillery should be stationed in the middle of Bermuda, able to rush to any threatened beach. From this idea came the eventual development of Prospect as a military camp.

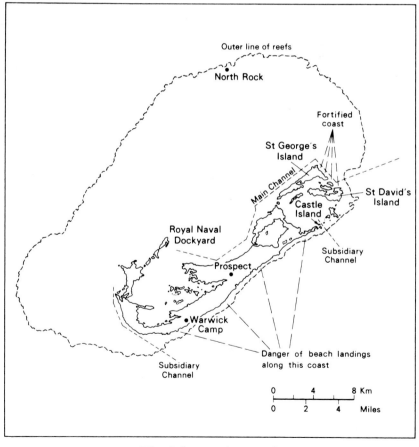

The defences of Bermuda

Apart from the massive fortifications which eventually were erected in response to the Duke's plan, the British also constructed the South Shore Road to assist in the defence of the beaches. At the tip of Ireland Island the Royal Navy erected a massive fortification known as the Keep with large warehouses with immensely strong roofs to keep gunpowder, shot and shell safe from accident or enemies. In the 1820s they also built a grandiose mansion for the Commissioner of the Dockyard – a building which soon became the object of jibes from British Army officers. One, Major Whittingham, declared that it was larger than any Government House anywhere in the Empire except India, and had stabling for 12 horses when the only way on and off the island was by boat. In fact the roof of the building is held up by cast-iron rafters and the handsome verandah by cast-iron pillars – one of the earliest uses of cast iron construction in the world. Nowadays the Keep contains the Bermuda Maritime Museum, with many fine displays about Bermuda and sea, including a series about the Royal Navy.

Convicts

The Commissioner came to Bermuda in the same year that convicts were first brought here. The convicts built the early forts at the Dockyard and many of the buildings. Many of the convicts came here rather than being hung, for in the last century in Britain many crimes were punishable by death. An alternative to the death sentence was 'transportation', which meant that prisoners were sent to the colonies to work on public works. Many were sent to Australia, where most of them stayed, but of the convicts who came to Bermuda all who survived returned except one, a Mr Facy, who went into the livery stable business.

The convicts were housed in old ships called convict hulks which swung at anchor off the Dockyard with the men confined below. The conditions were little better than the conditions aboard slave trading vessels, and about a quarter of the men died before the end of their sentences.

The convict system came to an end in 1863. Afterwards the forts were built, to a great extent, by the soldiers themselves. While it lasted the system gave employment to Bermuda's dwindling merchant marine, and in one sad case, in 1862, a Bermuda barque

A convict bulk

called the *Cedrine* sailed for England with 200 convicts aboard. The voyage went well until the *Cedrine* entered the English Channel. There a fog came up, and during the night she ran ashore on the Isle of Wight. The weather was calm and the tide was falling, so convicts and crew all escaped safely ashore, but the beautiful *Cedrine* was a total loss. Some of her cedar timbers were saved and used in repairing the roof of a nearby church.

The New Capital

It was at this period that the capital was moved from St George's to Hamilton. People living west of St George's had complained for years about the capital being situated at one end of Bermuda and on an island, and in 1790, during Governor Henry Hamilton's administration, moves were made to establish a town at Crow Lane. The town was named after Governor Hamilton, and grew rapidly, for it was a far more convenient port of entry than St George's.

It was not until 1811 that the first moves were made to shift the capital to the new town, and the change was not actually made until 1 January 1815, to the disgust of St Georgians but the delight of most other Bermudians.

British Soldiers

British soldiers and sailors had a considerable impact on Bermuda. They brought a breath of the outside world, new ideas and new ways of doing things. They gave a tremendous impetus to Freemasonry in Bermuda, and also the Friendly Societies, such as the Oddfellows (see Chapter 13).

Army regulations strictly limited the number of soldiers' wives who could be transported away from England by a regiment, and as a result many of the soldiers lived with Bermuda women – and were parted with them when the regiment was moved. There were unhappy scenes as the troopships pulled out, taking away the men from their Bermuda families.

When their terms of service ended some of the men were able to obtain discharges in Bermuda. It was also possible to buy oneself out of the services, but the price was steep and few could raise the

A scene on Hamilton waterfront in the 19th century;
the photograph was taken in 1868 but is more typical
of earlier times, as no steamships are shown

money. In later times men leaving the Army found their way into the Police Force and similar jobs.

The officers, too, had an impact. The Royal Bermuda Yacht Club, for instance, owes its start to the Army and Navy, and towards the end of the century, when tourism had started, the officers added considerably to the social life of the island.

Undoubtedly the large number of Britons stationed in Bermuda pulled the island closer to the United Kingdom and away from its former close connections with the American mainland, maintaining an Anglo-American balance in the island.

NOTES
1. Quoted in Zuill, *Bermuda Journey*, pp.255–7.
2. Smith, *Autobiography*, pp.195–7.

SOURCES

James, *The Naval History of Great Britain from the Declaration of War by France in 1793 to the accession of George IV.*

Walker, Mrs (ed. Dwight Franklin Henderson), *The Private Journal of Georgiana Gholson Walker, 1852–1865.*

A Field Officer (Major Whittingham) *Bermuda, a Colony, a Fortress and a Prison.*

Zuill, W.E.S., *Bermuda Journey.*

13

The Last Years of Slavery

On 1 August 1834 slavery came to an end in Bermuda. In the island it was a quiet, solemn day, a Friday, and all over Bermuda people went to church to give thanks that slavery was no more. On that day 4000 people on the island became free, and black people who were already free gained equal legal status with white people. From then on, with one exception, no public laws in Bermuda referred to black or white; but wills and legal agreements continued to make a difference between the races. Only in our own time has this been brought to an end, for although slavery was finished segregation continued, and even now we have by no means reached a time when the colour of a person's skin is ignored.

The battle against slavery was almost as old as the English slave trade, but it was not until the late 18th century that it gained its first victory. In 1772, in Britain, Lord Chief Justice Mansfield, hearing a case involving a black man, James Somerset, declared slavery to be 'so odious that nothing could be suffered to support it but positive law'. There were no such laws in England, and although the Chief Justice's finding only decided that Somerset's master could not make him go out of England, it in fact led to the ending of slavery in England, and an estimated 14 000 people gained their freedom.

Although the Somerset case led to slavery's end in Britain, in the colonies the situation was very different. There were many laws supporting the existence of slavery in the colonies, and so it remained. After a while, however, English consciences began to be pricked over the continuation of slavery in British territories overseas. Men such as Granville Sharp, first chairman of the Society for the Abolition of the African Slave Trade; William Wilberforce, who led the fight in Parliament; and Thomas Clarkson and Thomas Fowell Buxton all helped to fight the battle.

It was a long fight against the entrenched interests of the time, and it was not until 25 March 1807 that the slave trade was abolished for all English colonies. Then a stronger law was passed in 1811. During the next ten years conventions were signed with other countries, and after the final defeat of Napoleon in 1815 the Royal Navy was able to mount a formidable challenge to ships engaged in slaving.

Meanwhile in Britain the campaign was against slavery itself. Wilberforce continued to lead the abolition movement, aided by Buxton and backed by a large number of people with Christian consciences, particularly the Wesleyan Methodists. At the same time English economists were saying that it was bad business for Britain to follow the tradition of buying expensive West Indian slave-grown sugar when it could be bought cheaper elsewhere. Therefore some argue that slavery ended because it was bad business, but it is more likely that a mix of motives combining idealism and economics led to emancipation.

Finally on 23 August 1833 the British parliament passed a law freeing all slaves in all British colonies on 1 August 1834, providing £20 million as compensation for slave owners, and a period of apprenticeship for slaves during which they would continue to work for their former owners. The Bermuda and Antigua Parliaments rejected the apprenticeship scheme, and Emancipation Day brought absolute freedom. It also brought compensation of £128 240 7s 6d for Bermuda slave owners. The Bermuda parliament made a significant change at the same time that it passed a local emancipation act. It also increased the property qualifications for voting. Previously a man who owned £30 worth of property was able to vote. This was now raised to £60. Although the amount was never again increased, the property qualification remained in force until 1965, when the first act giving every adult the right to vote was passed.

No governmental thought either in Britain or Bermuda was given to the problems faced by the newly emancipated slaves adjusting to a different world – such problems as possible eviction from the slave quarters which had been their homes and, for children and the elderly, a lack of the support previously provided by owners. Whites, too, faced a new world, and one white Bermuda woman wrote in her private memoirs that her mother had said that the end of slavery had been the making of white men, who now had to work instead of lying back and expecting things to be done for them.

The white people in Bermuda were afraid that the black people would riot on Emancipation Day, but the *Royal Gazette* reported on the Tuesday after the event:

> Four days of universal freedom have now passed; and four days of more perfect order and regularity and quiet have these famed peaceful Isles never witnessed. In one instance only have we heard of anything like a general and public ebullition of feeling, and this consisted in those recently liberated in St George's meeting on the square in that town on Saturday morning, and giving three long and loud huzzas and then dispersing, each to his own home and occupation.

For years afterwards there was an annual celebration to commemorate Emancipation Day. Later it became traditional for the annual Cup Match between teams representing St George's and Somerset to take place at this time, and nowadays Emancipation Day has been remembered by a ceremony on the square in St George's.

Slavery In Its Last Years

It is difficult to reconstruct what life was like in a time past, for specific tales will often disprove broad generalizations. Written material by contemporaries coupled with anecdotes handed down through the generations will, however, give a flavour of a period with all its variations and complexities.

For Bermuda one pamphlet stands out. It was printed in 1831, three years before the end of slavery, by Thomas Pringle, the secretary of the Anti-Slavery Society, and was called *The History of Mary Prince*, a West Indian Slave. Mary Prince was in fact a Bermudian born into slavery, whose tale shows how varied the treatment of slaves could be and demonstrates how much they were at the mercy of their owners.

When she was a young girl Mary Prince was purchased by a Captain Darrell who presented her to his young granddaughter Betsy Williams, and her mother and other children to his daughter and son-in-law, Captain and Mrs Williams. The home was a happy one except when Captain Williams returned from his voyages. The family finances were at a low ebb and Mary was rented to a Mrs Pruden, who lived five miles away, to care for her infant son Daniel.

Then came tragedy. Mrs Williams died and Captain Williams married again. In order to support his new wife he decided to rid himself of some of his slaves, and Mary and her sisters were sent to the Vendue to be sold. It is a tragic and moving tale:

> We followed my mother to the market-place, where she placed us in a row against a large house, with our backs to the wall and our arms folded across our breasts. I, as the eldest, stood first, Hannah next to me, then Dinah; and our mother stood beside, crying over us. My heart throbbed with grief and terror so violently, that I pressed my hands quite tightly across my breast, but I could not keep it still, and it continued to leap as though it would burst out of my body. But who cared for that? Did one of the many by-standers, who were looking at us so carelessly, think of the pain that wrung the hearts of the Negro woman and her young ones? No, no! They are not all bad, I dare say, but slavery hardens white peoples' hearts towards the blacks, and many of them were not slow to make their remarks upon us aloud, without regard to our grief ... . Oh those white people have small hearts who can only feel for themselves.

The Vendue Master took Mary by the hand and took her into the middle of the street and 'exposed me to the view of those who attended ... .' She was surrounded by men 'who examined me and handled me in the same manner that a butcher would a calf or lamb he was about to purchase, and who talked about my shape and size in like words – as if I could no more understand their meaning than the dumb beasts.' She was sold for £57, to an owner who proved to be a sadistic bully married to a woman not much better. One day, Mary says, she was beaten by her master, referred to only as Captain I, so badly that she ran away to her mother. After hiding for some time her father, who was a sawyer who lived at Crow Lane and belonged to a Mr Trimingham who had a boat yard there, found her and returned her to Captain I. Mr Prince reproved Captain I for his conduct and Mary was not beaten that day – although she says that 'almost daily she received the same harsh treatment.'

What really happened? It may well be that Mary Prince ran away after being raped. Old stories hint at masters cohabiting with their defenceless female slaves, and indeed for them and for white women married to slave owners Emancipation Day had a special hidden meaning. It would not have been suitable in 1831 to refer to such an occurrence in a public pamphlet, but it would account for Mary's running away – although she gives a telling account of the thrashing she received. It is interesting to note, too, that even though her father was a slave he felt he could complain to Captain I about his behaviour.

Eventually, to Mary's great joy, she was sent to the Turks Islands to be sold, but it was a case of out of the frying pan, into the fire. She was purchased by Mr D who put her to work in the salt pans. They were filled with brine as the sun absorbed the water. As salt crystals appeared the slaves shovelled them into barrels and barrows and then took the salt and piled it into large heaps not likely to be affected by rain. D was a harsh master, quite prepared to whip his slaves and was aided and abetted by his son, Ben.

It was a dreadful life and continued for some years, when D decided to return to Bermuda leaving Ben in charge. He took Mary with him, and when they returned showed that his sadism was not reserved for slaves – his daughter suffered as badly as they.

> He had an ugly fashion of stripping himself naked, and ordering me to wash him in a tub of water. This was worse to me than all the licks. Sometimes when he called me to wash him I would not come, my eyes were so full of shame. He would then come and beat me.

Eventually Mary said she would no longer live with him for he was

> 'a very indecent man – very spiteful, and too indecent, with no shame for his servants, no shame for his own flesh. So I went away to a neighbouring house and sat down and cried till the next morning, when I went home again, not knowing what else to do.'

She was sent to work at another house, paying her wages over to her master on Saturday nights. Eventually she was hired to a Mr Wood who took her to Antigua, and then purchased her for £100. She did household work and cared for the Woods' child, and when they went away was left in charge of their house. In Antigua she encountered Moravian Christians and was taught to read.

Then Mary Prince met Daniel James, a carpenter and cooper, and fell in love with him. They were married in 1826 without the Woods' knowledge, which annoyed them, but Daniel was allowed to live in the back yard. Mary tried to buy her freedom, but the Woods would not sell.

Mary came to suffer severely from arthritis in Antigua, and when the Woods decided to pay a visit to England she asked to come with them in the hope her arthritis would get better, but it was not a successful choice. In England she learned that she could be free, and eventually ran away, ending up as a housemaid in the household of Mr Pringle. The Woods refused to sell her her freedom, so Mary could not return to her husband in Antigua, for there she would once more be the Woods' slave. At this point the narrative ends and it is not known whether she lived to see Emancipation and returned to Antigua or Bermuda.

There was a strong reaction in Bermuda when the pamphlet was published and an article in the *Royal Gazette* bears out Mary Prince's feelings about many white people. The article declared that : 'The Anti-Slavery Society lent a not unwilling ear to the statement of this woman,' adding 'and the result is the pamphlet before us, published under the editorship of the vilest description ... '. The Woods were praised as being highly respectable, and Mary Prince was described as a prostitute.

Other Views

Just before emancipation Harriett Suzette Lloyd, a visitor to Bermuda, penned a series of letters home to England which were later printed as a book. The population, she said, was about 10 000 people, half being black and half white. Of the black people 740 were free. She writes about three black teachers in Church of England schools. One, a slave, is only referred to as Maria, but another was a free woman named Sally Socco, and a third was a man, Mr Tankard. By the time of Miss Lloyd's visit the Church of England was attempting to catch up with the lead given by the Wesleyan Methodists in working with the people, and the employment of black teachers was an indication of this.

It was in 1800 that the Wesleyan missionary George Stephenson had been imprisoned for preaching, as he said, 'to African Black and captive Negroes'. In the next 25 years white attitudes changed, and in 1825 the Chief Justice, John Christie Esten, a man of liberal opinions, gave land at Cobbs Hill for a chapel to be built where slaves could worship. The work was undertaken by Edward Frazer, a slave. His owner, Francis Lightbourne, had brought him from Barbados. Frazer exhorted the black people of Warwick to work on the chapel, and men and women alike carried stone from nearby quarries to the building site. They could only work on moonlit nights and holidays, and the chapel took two years to complete. It still stands, a remarkable tribute to people who were willing to work together against odds to achieve their ends. In 1829 Lightbourne gave Frazer his freedom, and later Frazer went to England where he pleaded for the needs of black people.

Miss Lloyd, who helped found a Church of England school for black people, attempted to look at slavery in Bermuda from an overall viewpoint. 'It must be confessed,' she said,

> that in these islands slavery wears the mildest aspect of which that pitiable condition is susceptible. The character of the Bermudians is kind and humane, and their slaves enjoy many secular advantages of which the poor in our own country are frequently destitute ... Still, however ... the coloured inhabitants of Bermuda are bondsmen, and have long suffered the heaviest ills of bondage, a political incapacity to receive equal justice, and a spiritual privation of religious instruction and happiness.

At the same time that Mary Prince was suffering from being a slave of the Woods a group of Bermudian seamen decided to return home rather than take freedom in a strange land. In 1828 two Bermuda vessels with 12 slaves among the crew arrived at Belfast, Northern Ireland. The slaves were told that they could be free, and all except one, Thomas Albuoy, went before a magistrate. Joshua Edwards and Robert Edwards said they wanted to be free, but George Basset declared: 'I am obliged to the gentlemen for their offer of freedom but I wish to return to my friends'. The other eight questioned expressed much the same sentiments. They included Francis Ramie, Joseph Varman, James Lambert, John Stow and Joseph Rollin. The Belfast newspaper said of them:

> They are healthy, stout men, clean and well-clothed. They spoke English very well and conversed familiarly with different gentlemen in the courtroom. They said that in Bermuda their employment was not very laborious. They did some work on the Sabbath days, but not much ... they said they were usually hired out by their masters, who get two-thirds of their earnings, and they get the other third ... . They appeared to be content and happy, and when they spoke of returning to their families and friends their looks indicated the finest emotions of affection.

One wonders whether the writer would have said the same if they had come from the salt pans of the Turks Islands.

Just before Emancipation oral tradition tells of some owners who tried to sell their slaves off the island. Mrs Nellie E. Musson, in *Mind the Onion Seed*, tells of a mother successfully threatening her owner with an axe to save her family, and of the wife of a slave owner who hid the couples' slaves away from her husband.

Just after Emancipation, in February 1835, an important legal decision resulted in the freeing of 72 American slaves. They were aboard the brig *Enterprise* and had in fact been stolen from a Virginia plantation. The *Enterprise* put in to Bermuda for provisions and water, but before she sailed a Friendly Society, according to the *Royal Gazette*, obtained a writ of Habeas Corpus and despite pleas by the brig's captain that the writ be deferred until next morning, his request was denied and the slaves were brought ashore. At 9 p.m. they were brought into court. Each one was informed, individually, that they had the right to remain in Bermuda and be free, and all accepted except one woman with five children. A subscription was taken up to help them, and temporary lodging was found in a storehouse belonging to Mr W. M. Cox.

Fortifications and Agriculture

So the great change took place and slavery was over. But other changes were happening too. The period of shipbuilding and trading in ships was drawing to a close. Bermudians would continue owning ships and taking jobs as sailors for years to come, but the community was moving to a time when it could no longer rely on the sea for a living. Although Bermudians' connection with the Turks Islands continued, and continues to this day, the islands had been placed under the control of the Bahamas, and the trade in salt had declined in importance.

The steadily increasing fortification of Bermuda brought in a considerable income, but in 1839, with the arrival of Colonel William Reid as Governor, Bermuda started looking at the land. Governor Reid realized two things: that the commerce of Bermuda needed to be improved, and that it was vitally important that the island should be able to feed itself in case of war with America. He calculated that if war broke out the Royal Navy squadron might be away from Bermuda, which would mean that the American Navy could mount a successful blockade, and if sufficient food could not be grown on Bermuda, then Bermuda could be forced to surrender. Therefore he worked hard to persuade Bermudians to try agriculture, and succeeded so well that by 1851, some 12 years later, there were 104 ploughs on the island instead of the three Reid had found in 1839. Exports doubled in value, with Bermuda farmers exporting arrowroot, potatoes, onions, tomatoes and other vegetables.

Portuguese Settlers

It was about this time that the first Portuguese settlers came to Bermuda in some numbers. A few Portuguese arrived in Bermuda as part of the general migration of Portuguese people across the Atlantic to Massachusetts and parts of the West Indies, but in 1847 the Legislature voted £400 to be paid as a bounty to a vessel which brought in Portuguese settlers. In November 1849, Captain B. W. Watlington brought in 58 immigrants from Madeira aboard the barque Golden Rule and claimed the bounty.

Efforts to bring in more Portuguese continued spasmodically throughout the century, to be accelerated in the 1920s as the development of the tourist trade required more and more workers in the fields. The official importations came principally from the Azores, and the Portuguese were kept as much as possible to agricultural work. Nowadays their descendants are an integral part of the community, working in many trades and professions.

Departure of Governor Reid

During Governor Reid's administration the British Army started acquiring land to build the great camp at Prospect, home of the mobile reserve suggested in the Duke of Wellington's plan for the defence of Bermuda. Governor Reid left Bermuda in 1846, but his wisdom in preparing Bermuda for danger was shown a short 15 years later, when the Civil War broke out in America, and Britain and the Federal Government nearly declared war on each other.

Governor Reid, like Governor Butler, is known as one of Bermuda's good governors. Like Governor Butler, Bermuda was by no means the only place where he made his mark. Perhaps he is most remembered internationally for his remarkable deductions about hurricanes. Working on the basis of reports of hurricanes in different parts of the Caribbean and the East, he discovered that the same storm would pass from one place to another. He also worked out the circular nature of the storms and told captains of ships, for the first time, the best way to steer when they encountered the outer fringes of a hurricane. Much more is now known about hurricanes, but Reid's basic deductions are still sound.

Oddfellows

Although Friendly Societies were in existence earlier, the first recorded meeting of Oddfellows was called by Henry Thomas and took place in 1848. The Oddfellows are an international working man's movement founded in Britain. Members band together to pay subscriptions to the society, and the society, in turn, helps members in difficulties. Frequent meetings are held at which lodge members wear special regalia for rites and ceremonies. The Oddfellows movement came to Bermuda five years after it reached the United States, and the first lodges were part of the Grand United Order. By 1864 the movement was so popular that members took up all the carriages in St George's on the day there was a grand meeting in Hamilton. In 1879, with the added impetus of soldiers and sailors

Governor Sir William Reid

stationed here, a second group of lodges started under the banner of the Independent Order of Oddfellows.

Dancing and Songs

People took pleasure in simple things – often sitting around in an evening and swapping stories, or singing together, or listening to a friend play an instrument or recite. Harriett Suzette Lloyd tells of seeing Gombeys dancing at Christmas time in 1829. Their costume then was made with scarlet cloth, flowers, ribbons and red and yellow paints, and they sang as well as danced. The most famous Gombey groups, she said, were from Hamilton and Heron Bay, and as they marched down the road they were led by marching bands, the men dressed in neat white uniforms with scarlet facings.

> These musicians are all self-taught, and play many favourite airs with surprising accuracy. This is the more surprising as they do not know a single note of music. They learn and play everything by ear, and certainly have great natural taste, and love for music.

In the latter part of the century some of the dances had biblical themes, with dancers wearing headdresses depicting such things Noah's Ark. People sang as they walked along or worked, and a number of people played the flute or violin. Words were often made up to fit the music of popular songs and even of 'Italian airs', Miss Lloyd said.

One notable versifier of the day was a woman named Pliny [or Piny], and woe betide the man or woman who was made the object of her verses. The creating of popular verses continued well into the 20th century, and today there are still a number of Bermudians who like to write poetry.

It seems likely that the old parish verses date from the early 19th Century. Here are some of them:

St George's
The St George's people are so poor
They see you coming and slam the door.

Hamilton Parish
All the way to Bailey's Bay
Fish 'n' taters every day.

Devonshire
All the way to Brackish Pond
Cow-wheel soup and damaged corn.

Paget Parish
All the way to Crow Lane side,
Nothing there but foolish pride.

Sandys Parish
All the way to Mangrove Bay
There the old maids go to stay.

Were the verses made up by hungry Gombeys?

SOURCES
Gates Jr, *The Classic Slave Narratives.*
Gerzina, *Black England – Life before Emancipation.*
Lloyd, *Sketches of Bermuda.*
Mudd, *Portuguese Bermudians.*
Musson, *Mind the Onion Seed.*
Robinson, *Heritage.*
Zuill, W.E.S., *Bermuda Sampler.*
Zuill, W.E.S., *Bermuda Journey* (1st edition).

14

The Blockade of Bermuda

On 12 April 1861 Americans in the city of Charleston, South Carolina, opened fire on Americans in Fort Sumter in Charleston Harbour, and the American Civil War was on. It was a crisis which had been brewing for a very long time, and it was brought to a head by the election of President Abraham Lincoln, candidate of the anti-slavery Republican Party.

When the guns boomed across Charleston harbour Lincoln called for volunteers to keep the Union together. That was the official reason for the war, not slavery – that came later when Lincoln declared most of the slaves freed. In any case everyone assumed that slavery was the principal issue. Indeed, fear that the North would force an end of slavery on the South was the main reason why so many southern states seceded from the Union and formed the Confederate States of America. It was a long and bloody war, for the southerners proved to be able and canny soldiers who defended their newly formed country with fervour for four years against the attacks of the stronger Federal forces.

On 19 April 1861 Lincoln declared a blockade of southern ports, and the following year Bermuda was plunged into an exciting period which saw enormous changes in her way of life. The blockade cut off British mills from their main supplier of cotton, and cut off the Confederacy from European suppliers of arms, ammunition, clothing, medical supplies, manufactured goods and luxuries. In Europe the price of cotton soared, as did the prices of many things in the South. Anyone who could take goods in through the northern blockade and bring out cotton could make a fortune. At first it was easy to do this, but the Federal navy rapidly increased in size and efficiency, and blockade runners now needed to be specialized vessels. New steamships were built, mainly in British shipyards, which were small, low in the water and equipped with powerful engines.

Goods for the Confederacy were shipped out to Bermuda, Nassau, Havana and Matamoras, Mexico, in ordinary freighters, and were trans-shipped into the blockade runners which slipped into the southern ports and slipped out again with cotton which the freighters took back to Britain and Europe. St George's, a commercial backwater since it stopped being the capital, suddenly boomed as the freighters and blockade runners took advantage of its harbour close to the ocean. Money was to be made not only from the loading and unloading of goods bound back and forth but also from the crews as the sailors came ashore with hundreds of dollars in their pockets for making a single successful run.

Bermuda also had visits from Federal and Confederate warships, and two very odd incidents occurred during the war. The first warships to come were Northern vessels, and they met with a cool reception in Bermuda, for many people here tended to favour the Southern side which was causing the economic boom. It was not surprising: captains of blockade runners were paid $5000 in gold for a successful run in and out, and the rest of the crew were paid in proportion. Many of the captains were Royal Navy officers on leave; they helped to make the authorities partial to the Confederate side.

When the Confederate warship *Nashville* came in for supplies of coal the Federal Consul, C.M. Allen, protested that British regulations laid down that warships from the two opposing sides could only buy enough coal to take them to a home port, but officials said the regulations had not yet been made official. They had been made official, however, when the next warships arrived: the Federal ships *Wachusett*, *Sonoma* and *Tioga*. The squadron was commanded by Acting Rear-Admiral Charles Wilkes, a man who had already set London and Washington at odds when he removed the Confederate agents Mason and Slidell from a British ship. Only the coolness and common sense of President Lincoln and Prince Albert, Queen Victoria's consort, had averted war. Wilkes and Governor H. St George Ord were soon at loggerheads, each accusing the other of breaches of etiquette. To add insult to injury, Admiral Wilkes left the USS *Sonoma* outside the harbour to watch for blockade runners. She then entered port, obtained her ration of coal, and Admiral Wilkes ordered her and the *Tioga* to blockade Bermuda while he sailed the *Wachusett* south to the Bahamas. Bermuda, said the Admiral, was a 'nest of secessionists'.

The *Sonoma* and *Tioga* successfully frightened seven blockade runners so that they stayed in harbour, and then managed to fire a shot across the bows of the Royal Mail steamer *Merlin*. This infuriated the Governor but there was little he could do about it. Eventually the ships departed because their coal was running low.

Blockade running was an exciting business. A number of Bermudians served on the crews of the little ships, which would slip out of Bermuda and head for Wilmington, North Carolina. A careful lookout was kept for Federal warships, but the real excitement started as the ships neared the American coast, for there the blockading squadron drew a tight cordon around the entrance to the port. The approach was always made at night. All lights were extinguished, and sometimes canvas was hung over the paddle wheels to muffle their splashing. At slow speed the little ship approached land, never quite sure when a blockader might loom up out of the darkness. If she were spotted the engines would be revved up to full steam ahead while the stokers laboured to heap coal on the fires, as the skipper steered for the coast hoping to hide his ship against the shoreline.

Eventually, if she were lucky, the blockade runner would come under the protection of Confederate gun batteries, slip into the Cape Fear River and make her way up to Wilmington. There was always a desperate need for the cargo, which would be rapidly unloaded, to be replaced by a cargo of cotton. Finally the ship would slip down the river again, try to steam out to sea unseen and return to St George's.

Wilmington became a prime port for the Confederacy because there were two entrances to the Cape Fear River, making it more difficult to block, and because it was on the main north-south railway which linked Charleston and Savannah with Richmond, the capital and a vital manufacturing centre for the new nation.

Story of the Roanoke

The Confederates fought bravely, but slowly the power of the North took effect, and the Southerners were pressed back. This

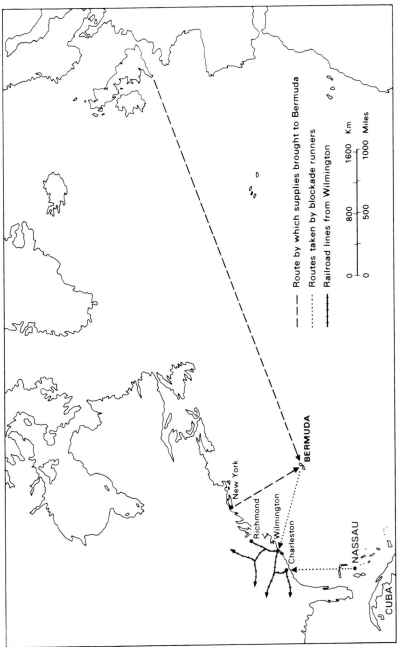

Routes of the blockade-runners during the American Civil War

Blockade-runners at anchor in St George's Harbour

resulted in some Southerners thinking up unusual ways to fight the war.

One of the methods was the brainchild of a man named John Clibbon Braine. Braine obtained a privateering licence – a letter-of-marque – from the Confederacy, but instead of purchasing a ship and going to sea to hunt Union shipping, he got together a gang and went to Havana. Late in 1864 they went aboard the US mail ship *Roanoke* as passengers. The first night out he and his gang overpowered the crew, shot the carpenter, wounded the third engineer, and set a course for Bermuda. He also rifled the safe of $21 000. It was a legal hijacking.

At Bermuda Braine anchored offshore, apparently fearing that the *Roanoke* would be detained if she entered port. He made arrangements for coal to be brought out to her, but found that, with a rolling sea, transferring coal in small boats from a collier brig was just about impossible. Instead, he sent the *Roanoke*'s passengers to Halifax in another brig, and decided to destroy the ship. On the evening of 8 October 1864 St Georgians were startled to see the *Roanoke* on fire in Five Fathom Hole. Soon afterwards Braine and his crew, including a Bermudian, R.E.N. Boggs, who had been hired to help take the ship to Wilmington, came ashore. They faced a brief court hearing, but Braine produced his letter-of-marque, and all were released.

Yellow Fever Plan

Another Confederate scheme, a horrifying one, came to light in the spring of 1865 when the Confederacy was on its last legs. Dr Luke P. Blackburn was an able doctor who arrived in Bermuda from Halifax late in 1864 during a yellow fever epidemic.

Yellow fever was a fearful problem in Bermuda during much of the 19th century, periodically raging through the island and killing large numbers of people. We know now that it is transmitted from one person to another by a mosquito, the *Aedes aegyptii*, which has now been eliminated from the island. In those days, however, no one knew how the fever was passed on. Particular sufferers were people newly arrived from countries which had few or no mosquitoes, like Britain, and sometimes regiments sent here on garrison duty were decimated by the disease on arrival. A plaque in St Peter's Church tells a dreadful tale of the losses of one regiment, and a memorial in the main military cemetery in St George's tells about other deaths.

Dr Blackburn said he had special knowledge of the disease, and volunteered his services free of charge. People were glad to see him and he worked hard among the victims. What people did not know was that when he offered to dispose of what was thought to be infected clothing, blankets and sheets, he was in fact storing them. He hired a man named Swan to look after his trunks and his plan was to distribute them among the poor of New York and other big northern cities during the coming summer in the hope of causing an epidemic.

Blackburn left Bermuda, and while he was gone word about the diabolical scheme reached US Consul Allen, who told the St George's Health Officer, who in turn told the Corporation of St George's. One member of the Corporation was a Southern sympathizer, and he signalled to a Confederate spy outside the window. But the other members were too quick. Suspecting what was going on, they appointed a committee to search the suspected house, and reached it just as Swan was about to set fire to the offending articles.

Swan was sent to prison for 'harbouring a nuisance' and the clothing was carefully destroyed. Years after the war, in 1879, Dr Blackburn was elected Governor of Kentucky. To be fair to the doctor, he was known for his thought for others and before, during and after the war often gave his services against yellow fever free of charge.

Victory for the North

By this time the war was over as far as Bermuda was concerned. On 15 January 1865 Fort Fisher, which guarded the main channel into the Cape Fear River, fell to Northern troops. There was consternation in Bermuda. Merchants who had imported goods to send through the blockade or had stocked their shops with articles for sale to the rich crews of the blockade runners, found that trade simply ceased. The blockade runners and adventurers melted away, and for years afterwards the merchants shouldered a fearful burden of debt.

The end of the war was good news for one man in St George's. He was Joseph Hayne Rainey of South Carolina. Before the war Rainey's father had purchased his own and his family's freedom, and set up in business as a barber in Charleston. When fighting started the Charleston authorities drafted all free black men to work on the fortifications. Rainey escaped and with his wife came to Bermuda. (One tale says they came on a blockade runner, with Rainey acting as steward). Once in Bermuda they set up in business, Rainey as a barber (although at one point he was a bar tender at the Hamilton Hotel) and his wife as a dressmaker under the name of Madame Elise.

It is generally believed that Mrs Rainey had trained under Madame Demarest of New York, who was noted for hiring seamstresses whatever their origin and background, and for using paper patterns – the first person to do so. There are, however, indications that it was the future Mrs Rainey who invented the paper pattern idea and taught Mme Demarest. Madame Elise was an able seamstress and quickly became a leading dressmaker in Bermuda, even making a splendid evening gown for Mrs Norman Walker, wife of the Confederate Agent (Mrs Walker used a friend of the same size as a go-between).

Rainey himself set to work to improve his education. Some of his customers gave him a hand, marking his workbooks. He took an interest in Bermuda and became a member of the Independent

Order of Oddfellows, Manchester Unity, putting his signature to a document commiserating with the United States on the assassination of President Lincoln. He may have been a Union secret agent, for he gave evidence in the case against Swan and said that he had travelled to Halifax in the same ship as Blackburn.

In 1866 the Raineys returned to South Carolina and during the Reconstruction period (when black people and Northern sympathizers held political power in the South, protected against white threats by the Federal army) he became the first black man to be sworn in as a member of the US House of Representatives. His speeches show that he was a wise man with great vision, an able debater, and a person who demonstrated that he held no grudge against the former slave-owners.

After the Hayes-Tilden election, which, through political skulduggery, made the Republican Rutherford Hayes President but forced the Republicans to agree to withdraw the US Army from the South, white mobs and secret societies like the Ku Klux Klan took control and the civil rights gained by African-Americans after the end of the war were abrogated. Rainey lost his seat and afterwards made a living at various government jobs while Mrs Rainey helped support the family by making fashionable hats. They went to live in Windsor, Connecticut, where Mrs Rainey is buried.

At the end of the war Major and Mrs Norman Walker fled to England where he went into business. They returned to the United States many years later and took up residence on Staten Island. Mrs Walker wrote a diary which reflected a fervent patriotism for a newly formed nation and which gives a wonderful if biased picture of Bermuda during the war years.

The Curious Raft

Some years after the war a group of St David's Islanders sitting on a hillside overlooking the sea observed a curious wreck floating offshore. Interested, they took a boat out to it and found an enormous raft, certainly worth dragging ashore for the timber and fastenings.

They obtained help and brought the hulk into Dolly's Bay. Then they tried to take it apart, but so strongly was it built that they could not make any progress. They could not even set fire to it. So they abandoned it. Years later Captain E.H. Faucon of the US

Navy happened to spot the raft. He remembered it immediately. It was one of three which his ship, the *Ericson* had attempted to tow to Charleston Harbour with the idea of using them in a naval attack on the harbour. Off Cape Hatteras a gale hit and the raft broke away. Attempts to find it failed, and it had drifted for six years before the St David's Islanders dragged it to shore. At the time of writing parts of it are still to be seen.

The one raft to survive the tow around Cape Hatteras reached Charleston and was fitted to the bow of an ironclad, where it was tied on with heavy ropes. It was thought that if it hit any mines (called torpedoes then) they would explode without damaging the ironclad. Unfortunately when the ship and tow encountered the steep seas at the bar at the entrance to Charleston Harbour the raft battered the ship so dangerously that the idea was abandoned.

SOURCES
Anderson, *From the Steeple*.
Hayward, *Bermuda Past and Present* (revised edition).
Musson, *Mind the Onion Seed*.
Packwood, *Detour – Bermuda, Destination – U.S. House of Representatives*.
Walker, Mrs (ed. Dwight Franklin Henderson), *The Private Journal of Georgiana Gholson Walker, 1852–1865*.
Wilkinson, *Bermuda from Sail to Steam*.
Zuill, W.E.S., *Bermuda Journey* (1st edition).

15

A Time of Peace

At the end of the American Civil War European statesmen suddenly realized that they faced a great military power on the other side of the Atlantic, a United States with an enormous army of veterans and a large and capable navy, all armed with the latest weapons. However, European fears were unnecessary: Americans breathed a great sigh of relief that the ordeal was over and turned their attention to such vast civilian projects as completing the first trans-Continental railroad line. They did prevent France from continuing to use her soldiers to support the Mexican Empire of Maximilian, and this may have misled Europeans for a time as to the intentions of this great new power.

For Bermudians the fears were reflected in a big increase in fort building, and in the stationing here of large contingents of the British Army and Navy. It was a scale of fortification which continued to the end of the century, with further improvements necessitated by rapid scientific improvements in gunnery and ships. The building and rebuilding of the forts brought large sums of money into Bermuda and helped support the economy.

Fort Catherine is one of the earliest forts of this period, standing boldly at the end of the Narrows Channel, just at the point where an enemy ship would turn the headland and come in sight of the Dockyard. The last permanent British fort built in Bermuda was St David's Battery. Armed with breech loading guns, it was an important part of the colony's fortifications until the end of the Second World War.

Fort Hamilton – a good example of a 19th century British fort, now open to the public

Agriculture

The last half of the 19th century was a comparatively quiet time for Bermuda. Despite the fort building, the western Atlantic was free of war, and was to remain so for nearly fifty years. The island for a time lay outside the mainstream of world affairs. Apart from the military bases, agriculture dominated the economy. Bermuda onions became particularly famous in New York, with £85 548 worth being exported in 1897. This was why Bermudians came to be known as 'Onions'. Potatoes were another important crop, arrowroot yet another. Bermuda arrowroot at one time was held to be the best in the world, but as with other agricultural efforts here, larger places elsewhere were eventually able to outproduce and undersell Bermudian products. Even the Bermuda onion went under, succumbing to Texas growers and increasing customs duties in the United States. The final export was the Easter lily, which continued to be sold abroad for many years after the Second World War.

Bermuda was such a quiet place during the 19th century that a number of people emigrated, principally to the United States, and nowadays many Bermuda families have relations there. Yet despite the quietness important steps were being taken. In May 1883, the first black man was elected to the House of Assembly. He was William Henry Thomas Joell, a carpenter, and he was elected to serve as a Member for Pembroke. Four years previously he was one of the persons who met to found the Berkeley Educational Society (see Chapter 22). The others were:

- John Henry Thomas, a schoolmaster;
- Richard Henry Duerden, a drygoods merchant and auctioneer;
- Samuel David Robinson, a baker;
- Eugenius Charles Jackson, a lawyer;
- Charles William Thomas Smith, a physician;
- William Orlando F. Bascome, a dentist;
- John Henry T. Jackson, who later on became a Member of the Colonial Parliament (MCP as members were known);
- Samuel Parker and his son of the same name, printers, publishers and proprietors of the first black newspaper, the *Times and Advocate*; and
  Henry T. Dyer, a ferry-boat man.

Roman Catholic and AME Churches

George Stephenson of the Wesleyan Methodists had broken the dominance of the Church of England and the Church of Scotland in Bermuda, and in 1820 the first Roman Catholic priest, Father Boland, arrived. He came by accident when the sailing vessel he was aboard put into Bermuda in distress. Father Boland stayed for two months, and was supported by members of the 37th Regiment stationed here. The first resident priest, however, did not arrive in Bermuda until 1846. In that year the Rev. Dr. Michael Hannan came from Halifax and stayed for six months. Two years later the visit of the Most Rev. William Walsh, Bishop of Halifax, marked the official start of the Catholic Church in Bermuda.

The first Catholic church, St Edwards, was started in 1858 and on 15 April 1859, Easter Sunday, mass was celebrated in a completed section. The first presbytery was build in 1888. Another important church, the African Methodist Episcopal, dates its beginning to 1879 when Bishop Nazery came to Bermuda. The first AME service was held in the home of Mr John Burchall Benjamin of Park Gate, St George's. At first the church was a branch of the British Methodist Episcopal Church of Canada, but soon became a part of the AME Church of the United States. The first cornerstone of an AME church, St John's in Bailey's Bay, was laid on 16 October 1879. The largest AME church, St Paul, was dedicated in December 1881.

Public Buildings

It was during the 19th century that many of today's important public buildings were erected. The Sessions House, which contains the House of Assembly chamber and the principal court, was started in 1815 and was at first a large rectangular Bermuda-style building. In 1887 Bermuda wanted to find a way in which to commemorate Queen Victoria's Jubilee. The tourist trade had started, and visitors were comparing Bermuda to Italy, so the legislature decided to give a Florentine facade to the Sessions House; the plan was carried out using designs sketched by the Governor, Lieutenant-General Sir T.J.L. Galwey. Included in the plan were two towers, and a clock was ordered from Gillett and Johnson of Croydon, England.

The cornerstone of the Public Buildings, later known as the Secretariat and now the Cabinet Office, was laid on 8 May 1833, and the building was finished in 1836. Many people think it is the most dignified of Hamilton's public buildings. Hamilton's great Gothic Anglican cathedral was started in 1886 on the site of the ruins of a church which had burnt down in 1884. The plans for the cathedral were drawn by those architects to so many parts of the British Empire, Hay & Henderson of Edinburgh, and the exterior was finally completed in 1910, although further additions have been made to the building in our own time.

Another great building was the Colonial Opera House. It was designed by Bermudian William (Sike) Smith, who oversaw its building and completion, in 1908. Started in 1905 by the Oddfellows, who still own the site, the building was severely damaged in the hurricane of 1926, but was later restored. It was Bermuda's largest auditorium, and many a theatrical production graced its boards. In between it was used as a movie theatre. Finally it became the New Testament Church of God, and then tragically burnt down.

A notable American author and travel writer, William Dean Howells, writing in the early 1900s, declared:

> The two most beautiful buildings in Hamilton are the Cathedral, designed by an eminent Scottish architect and the Opera House, built by Bermudian Negroes, with labour and material they gave without cost, and fashioned after the plans of a colonial carpenter and mason. The Cathedral is very good modern Gothic; but the Opera House is like a bit of 16th century Rome, the unpolished coral rock shining like travertine, grayish yellow and endearingly soft to the eye. The contractor and mason had read some books about Greek and Roman architecture, but he had never been off his Island, and he had felt that beauty tenderly and delicately out with his head and his heart, so that it is a pleasure to look at it.[1]

Another building of the period is Gibbs Hill Lighthouse, a circular iron tower which when built measured 133 feet 9 inches from the ground to the top of the weathervane, now replaced by a radar scanner. It was designed by London civil engineer, Alexander Gordon, and erected under the direction of Lieutenant Colonel Philip Barry of the Royal Engineers between 1844 and 1846.

Gibbs Hill Lighthouse, a graceful example of
Victorian engineering

Tourist Trade

On 29 January 1883 Princess Louise, daughter of Queen Victoria and wife of the Marquess of Lorne, Governor General of Canada, came to Bermuda to spend the winter, and from that date the tourist business, apart from wartime interruptions, became a mainstay of the economy. In the 1880s, when travel was by slow steamer, Bermuda was one of the closest countries with a warm climate which could be reached easily from Canada and the northern part of the United States. Only later, with the development of air travel after the Second World War, did warmer islands further south become preferred to Bermuda for winter holidays, and Bermuda's high season switched to the spring, summer and autumn.

Even before the Revolutionary War people came here for various illnesses, for Bermuda even then had a reputation for its climate. The memorial to Governor Alured Popple (died 1744), in St Peter's Church, refers to '… the many who resorted thither for their health …' and there are other occasional references to visits here. Unfortunately some came because they suffered from 'consumption' which today we call tuberculosis, and although the balmy climate may have helped, the high humidity did not. It was not until many years later that long stays in dry Alpine resorts or in desert towns like Phoenix, Arizona, brought help to some patients.

The tourist trade was of long standing when it was given its first major impetus with the building of the Hamilton Hotel by the Corporation of Hamilton. It was recommended by the then Mayor, Henry J. Tucker, in 1851, and was finally completed in 1863. The scheme led to the building of other smaller establishments, which sufficed until Princess Louise came and Bermuda's popularity soared. The need for accommodation was met by the building of the second large hotel, called the Princess with the permission of Her Highness, which opened in 1885. The hotel has continued in business to this day, and now works in tandem with a sister resort, the Southampton Princess.

The hotel has had various owners through the years, including the American shipping magnate Mr Daniel Ludwig. He was obviously entranced by the name 'Princess' for he used it for other hotels in such places as the Bahamas and Acapulco, and also for some of his other interests, such as mines in Australia. In this odd way Princess Louise's visit to Bermuda has spread to many parts of the world. The Princess herself stayed at 'Inglewood', the Paget home of Mr James Trimingham. Her arrival caused an enormous stir, for Bermudians, whose loyalty had been severely shaken during the American Revolutionary War and was in doubt as late as 1850, were by now, as far as one can make out, devoted to Britain and the Crown, and Queen Victoria's daughter was the first Royal Princess to visit the island.

*Views of Hamilton at the end of the 19th century,
when the Hamilton and Princess hotels were built*

One tale about the Princess is that when she was out on one of her frequent walks she stopped at a small cottage to ask for a drink of water. The lady of the house said she was too busy ironing a shirt which she had to finish immediately as she was off next day to St George's to see the Princess. The Princess offered to iron the shirt while the woman fetched the water, but the housewife doubted the skill of her unknown visitor.

The visitor asked if she had seen the Princess, and the housewife said she had. Would she know her again? The housewife was not sure. 'Well,' said the visitor, 'take a good look at me now so that you will be sure to know me tomorrow at St George's, for I am the Princess.'

The housewife was overwhelmed, and while she went to get the water the Princess finished ironing the shirt.

Bermuda received a tremendous amount of publicity in the United States and Canada as a result of the Princess's visit, and numbers of people decided that if the island was good enough for a Princess it was good enough for them, too. Another notable visitor of the time was Mark Twain, the American humourist. It was he, after a trip to Bermuda across the turbulent Gulf Stream, who coined the phrase: 'Bermuda is paradise but you have to go through Hell to get to it.'

Boer War

There were a few years of excitement for Bermuda during the Boer War at the turn of the century. This was fought in South Africa with Britain on one side and the Boer Republics of Orange Free State and the Transvaal (now part of the Republic of South Africa) on the other. The British Government decided to send a number of Boer prisoners away from South Africa during the war. Bermuda had a garrison which was not involved in the fighting, and it seemed a good idea to make use of the troops as guards.

The War Office decided to use the West India Regiment to supplement the garrison. When they arrived the British troops were given the task of guarding the Boers while the West Indians took over garrison duties. The presence of the West India Regiment exposed a number of Bermudians to a wider world, and strengthened the ties between Bermuda and Caribbean.

The first Boer prisoners arrived here on 28 June 1901. Before the end of the war thousands were living on islands in Great Sound. A number of Bermudians felt sorry for the prisoners and helped them. Many of the Boers were excellent carvers, and there are still a large numbers of cedar souvenirs around the island which were made by these men. Another relic is the Boer cemetery and memorial pylon on Long Island.

When the war ended in 1902 most of the prisoners went home, and Bermuda settled back into a period of quiet.

Preparations for World War

By now, however, war clouds were gathering in Europe and the importance of the Bermuda base began to diminish. The Pacific, South Atlantic and the North America and West Indies squadrons were abolished, and instead one squadron, the Fourth Cruiser Squadron, took their place. Bermuda lost its admiral, the station being put under a captain-in-charge. Early in 1914, however, trouble in the Caribbean led to the Fourth Cruiser Squadron's being ordered to Bermuda on a semi-permanent basis. In command was Rear-Admiral Sir Christopher Cradock, whose arrival meant that the station was once more important enough to rate an admiral. Sir Christopher and two of his cruisers, the *Monmouth* and *Good Hope*, were soon to meet a heroic fate (see next chapter), for war was imminent. Britain declared war on Germany on 4 August 1914.

Song Of The Keepers Of The Western Gate

An idea of Bermudian patriotic feeling at the time of the First World War is shown in the verses of Miss Bessie Gray called 'Song of the Keepers of the Western Gate'. They are an expression of Bermuda's feeling for Britain.

> Queen of the Seas,
> Thou hast given us the keys:
> Proudly do we hold them, we thy lovers and akin.
> We will guard the Water-gate
> Though we be not strong or great
> And our lives shall pay the forfeit ere we let the foeman in.
>
> Empty are our hands,
> For we have not wealth nor lands

No grain of gold to give thee: and so few a folk are we
But in very will and deed
We will serve thee at thy need,
And keep they ancient fortalice above the Western Sea.

Mighty sons thou hast begot
Who have cast with thee their lot;
Thy quarrels are their quarrels, and thy rights their rights
    to guard.
We can only stand and wait
Making strong the Water-gate
That we be not found unready when the battle is toward.

The sea is at our doors
And we front its fretted floors,
Swept by every wind that listeth, ring'd with reefs from rim
    to rim.
Though we may not break its bars
Yet by light of sun or stars
Our hearts are fain for England, and for her our eyes are dim.

Sweet Mother, ponder this
Lest thy favour we should miss,
We, the loneliest and least of all the peoples of the Sea:
With bared head and proud
We bless thy name aloud
For gift of lowly service, as we guard the Gate for thee.

NOTE
1. Rider (ed.), *Rider's Bermuda*, p.64.

SOURCES
Gray, *A Bermuda Garden of Song.*
Harris, *Bermuda Forts.*
Hayward, *Bermuda Past and Present* (revised edition).
Musson, *Mind the Onion Seed.*
Robinson, *Heritage.*
Wilkinson, *Bermuda from Sail to Steam.*
Zuill, W.E.S., *Bermuda Journey* (1st edition).

16

Global War

When the British Empire went to war Rear-Admiral Sir Christopher Cradock had two things to worry about: blockading German ships in American and other neutral ports so that they could not go back home, and catching German warships so as to keep them from attacking allied vessels. Sir Christopher knew of two German light cruisers, the *Dresden* and the *Karlsruhe*, in his area, and soon after the war started he nearly caught the second one, but she was faster than his own vessel and escaped. Three months later there was an accident aboard her and she blew up and sank. The German Admiralty ordered the *Dresden* to go down the coast of South America and sail into the Pacific. This area was also part of the responsibility of the Bermuda base, and Sir Christopher followed.

Later in the year there were further worries for the Bermuda headquarters when it was learned that Vice-Admiral Maximilian Reichsgraf von Spee had left the China station with most of his squadron and was headed for the Americas. It was thought that he might even attempt to bring his ships through the newly opened Panama Canal, if the Americans would let him, and attack shipping in the Caribbean and Bermuda area. In fact he steamed for the coast of South America, and it was there, on 10 October 1914, that Admiral Cradock met him with an inferior squadron. The battle was disastrous for the British as the armoured German cruisers *Scharnhorst* and *Gneisenau* hammered away at the British *Monmouth* and *Good Hope*, sinking both of them. Sir Christopher died with his men, for there were no survivors.

The defeat had reverberations around the world, and fears as to the next move of the German cruisers permeated as far north as Bermuda. Sir Christopher, a bluff and hearty sailor, had made many friends while he was in the island, and the loss of his ships, with men aboard who had friends here, led to the Imperial Order, Daughters of the Empire, setting up as a memorial in his honour a scholarship which they still administer. There is also a Cradock Road at Ireland Island.

Admiral von Spee, who had nothing but admiration for his defeated foe, himself met defeat at the hands of Admiral F.C.D. Sturdee in the Battle of the Falkland Islands on 8 December 1914. Sturdee, with the powerful battlecruisers *Inflexible* and *Invincible*, sank von Spee's squadron, the German Admiral going down with his ships.

The Pollockshields Rescue

The next excitement for Bermudians came in 1915, when a former German merchantman, captured by the British and put to work for the allies, ran on the breakers off Elbow Beach, Paget. There was a hurricane nearby: the weather was thick and heavy and hurricane waves pounded across the reefs and high up on the beach. The problem was how to get the men ashore before the ship broke up. Antoine (Tony) Marshall, a whaleboat skipper and an experienced seaman, appeared on the scene. He suggested bringing his heavy whaling gig across the land from Waterlot Inn. Fired with enthusiasm, a gang of men went across to the anchorage at Waterlot while a messenger went to Hamilton to obtain the use of Mr Spurling's big horse-drawn dray, for there were no motor vehicles on the island – the Legislature had banned them a few years earlier when a motorcar called 'The Scarlet Runner' had frightened a horse so that it bolted. It took hours, in the gale force winds, for the horse to drag the dray from Hamilton to Waterlot. Meanwhile Marshall and his friends had worked hard and pulled the gig ashore.

The *Pollockshields* ran ashore early in the morning of 6 September. It was not until 3 a.m. on 7 September that the dray with gig aboard set out from Waterlot. Cheered on by Miss Claudia Darrell, who owned the Inn and provided food and drink for the workers, the expedition slowly worked its way to Elbow Beach.

Overhanging boughs had to be cut and the horse helped over the hills, and it was 8 a.m. before the gig was ready to be launched.

There was a furious sea, and Marshall and his crew – Edward Dillworth, Charles de Shield, Gordon Bascome, David Williams, Tom Basden and Reginald Minors – set out. On their first try the gig was turned over, end over end, and was thumped back on the beach, bottom up. The men were helped ashore and courageously jumped aboard again to have another try. This time they succeeded, and in four trips brought off the entire crew, except the captain. He had gone aft to try and rescue the ship's cat and kittens, but was swept overboard and drowned. For a fifth time Tony Marshall and his crew went out – and rescued the cat and kittens.

Bermudians in France

Before the war began Bermudians had started their own military corps of volunteers, and in 1914 the soldiers went on a war footing. The two corps were the Bermuda Militia Artillery (black) and the Bermuda Volunteer Rifle Corps (white). At first the men did garrison duty in Bermuda, the BMA helping to man the big guns in the many forts, while the BVRC were an infantry unit. Over in France, however, the casualty lists were growing longer and longer and Britain looked to her Empire for help, and so men from both units went over. The BVRC were attached to the Lincolnshire Regiment, while the BMA group, the Bermuda Contingent of the Royal Garrison Artillery (BCRGA) joined the Royal Artillery and worked in dangerous ammunition dumps just behind the front lines. There were many casualties, and many Bermudians never returned from the cold and muddy fields of Flanders to their warm island home. When there was heavy fighting in zones where Bermudians were stationed the two newspapers would race each other to set the grim telegrams in type and get the latest news to the people waiting in the street to learn something about their loved ones. Even worse were the casualty lists, with the news arriving by cable of the names of the dead. At that time the cable line from Halifax to Bermuda and the Turks Islands was the main link Bermuda had with the outside world, and with no radio or television stations, the newspapers were the only way people would learn the news.

A total of 360 Bermudians went overseas with the British Army, and of these over 40 never returned. Numbers of other Bermudians served in other branches of the British and Empire forces, and in the US forces, and also suffered casualties.

Official Appreciation

Bermuda's contribution was appreciated in England. One of the official reports on Bermuda's soldiers was written by Field Marshal Lord Haig, the Commander-in-Chief of the British Armies in France. He said of the Bermuda Militia Artillery:

> This contingent served with the Canadian Corps during the operations of May and June subsequent to the capture of Vimy Ridge. They were employed on Heavy Ammunition dumps and great satisfaction was expressed with their work. Though called upon to perform labour of the most arduous and exacting nature at all times of the day and night, they were not only willing and efficient but conspicuous for their cheeriness under all conditions. Their officers rendered valuable service in the management of the dumps.
>
> This unit also worked on ammunition dumps from the end of June to the beginning of September in another Corps. On more than one occasion the dumps at which they were employed were ignited by hostile shell fire. Their behaviour on all these occasions was excellent and commanded the admiration of those with whom they were serving. In fact the manner in which they carried on their work under all conditions was strikingly good.

Of the BVRC Lord Haig wrote:

> I desire to record my high appreciation of the gallantry and devotion shown by the Bermuda Contingent, and to endorse fully all the General Officer Commanding the Division says in regard to their distinguished record of service.

The Division's General said:

> Owing to casualties this contingent has now practically ceased to exist, and I wish to put on record my appreciation of the splendid services rendered by them ...

Five men have been awarded the Military Medal for gallantry in action, and one man, Private Noble, was promoted to Sergeant in the field by his Commanding Officer for gallantry in action on 3rd July 1916. Private Noble was unfortunately killed later on the same day.

The Bermuda Contingent has been in every action in which the battalion of the Lincolnshire Regiment to which they were attached has taken part in 23rd June 1915 … . In addition … they have done almost continuous duty in the trenches. They have at all times displayed great gallantry and devotion to duty.

Shipping Problems

One of the big problems Bermuda faced during the war was lack of shipping. The principal link between Bermuda and New York was provided by the Quebec Steamship Company's two liners, *Trinidad* and *Bermudian*. The *Bermudian* was withdrawn for war service early in 1914, but was later put back on the run and the *Trinidad* withdrawn. In June 1917, with German submarine sinkings mounting, the *Bermudian* was again pulled off the run, and a tiny ship called the *Cascapedia* was put in her place.

The SS Bermudian

The *Cascapedia* was completely inadequate for the job (she sometimes took six days to make the voyage) and she was finally replaced by the *Charybdis*, which had been a Royal Navy cruiser, but had hit another ship and damaged her bow and had been sent to Bermuda. Here the Dockyard had given her a new bow made of teak, but she was left lying alongside, retired from the war. With the consent of the Admiralty the Bermuda Government took her over and sent her to New York, where she was converted into a combined freight and passenger carrier. The *Charybdis* took over the run for the rest of the war and for some months after the Armistice of 11 November 1918.

American Base

On 6 April 1917 the United States declared war on Germany, and soon American ships began using Bermuda as a base. A year later, on 15 April 1918, the American Navy formally set up Base 24 in the Great Sound at Morgan and Tucker's Islands, and from here they supplied convoys of small submarine chasers which were steaming across the Atlantic to the war zone. In the weeks immediately following the end of the war a strange ghost ship steamed into Bermuda. She was the coal-burning tramp SS *Normandier*, and her last port had been Dakar. Dakar was in the grip of a dreadful form of malaria known as blackwater fever, and soon after the *Normandier* set out on her voyage to Halifax the crew started coming down with the illness. The ship had no doctor and only ordinary medical supplies, and the crew began to lapse into comas and die. Finally the last two persons able to drag themselves about the vessel were First Mate Ingleson and wireless operator H.L. Tredree. Though both were desperately ill, they succeeded in raising enough steam to work the dynamo to provide electricity to transmit messages, and finally two US and one British warship came to their aid. The lives of Tredree and Ingleson and several others of the crew were saved.

Before the US Navy gave up their Bermuda base an American ship named the *Elinore* came to the island with the first aircraft Bermudians had ever seen. It was described as a 'naval scout hydroaeroplane' – in other words a seaplane – and its pilot, Ensign G. L. Richards, took up Governor General Sir James Willcocks for a spin on 22 May 1919. This was the first airplane flight that ever took place here.

During that same year the optimistic Bermuda West Atlantic Aviation Company was started by Major Harold Kitchener who looked forward to transatlantic flights. He was twenty years before his time, however, and although he and his associates ran an aerial sightseeing business and took a number of Bermudians up for flights, the company suffered financial failure. The attempt was, however, symbolic of the start of the new era for Bermuda which Armistice Day brought in. Armistice Day itself, though still remembered with a public holiday every year, is now part of our past. At the time it symbolized the dawn of a new hope for mankind, the end of the 'war to end all wars' – a hope which did not materialize.

SOURCES
Hayward, *Bermuda Past and Present* (revised edition).
Tredree, *The Strange Ordeal of the Normandie*.
Zuill, W.E.S., *Bermuda Journey* (1st edition).

17

Tourism

One sign of the public mood at the end of 'the war to end all wars' was the decision of the United States to ban the sale of liquor. It was a decision democratically arrived at, but many Americans disagreed with it. However, Prohibition helped the Bermuda tourist trade, for Bermuda did not follow suit. For a time, however, Bermuda had a law prohibiting the export of liquor to the United States, but this was allowed to expire at the end of 1925 and rum-running, which was akin to the blockade-running of the Civil War days, became legal. Vessels left Bermuda and sailed to New York, where they anchored just outside the territorial limits, staying for a week or more, selling liquor to anyone who ventured out in a boat. The trade had its dangers since occasionally groups of gangsters would attempt to hijack ships because the profits could be considerable. It has a strong resemblance to the drug trafficking of today.

In this way money came into Bermuda and helped keep the community going, but the importance of Prohibition to the island lay mainly in the encouragement it gave to the tourist trade, which became Bermuda's major industry. It was the British Furness, Withy shipping company which played a large role in the development of tourism. Back in 1875 the small Quebec and Gulf Ports Steam Ship Company successfully answered a Bermuda government call for tenders to provide a 500-ton ship to run between New York and Bermuda at least once every three weeks. Between then and 1917 the company succeeded in more than filling the requirements. Starting with the *Canima*, 246 feet long, the company brought increasingly larger ships on the run, so that by 1907 their passenger accommodation had increased by 700 per cent, the tonnage of their ships on the run by 400 per cent, and the speed of their vessels 100 per cent. During that time the channels into Bermuda were improved and, most important for Hamilton, Two-Rock passage was dredged so that large ships no longer had to wait for the tide to be high enough to pass through Timlins Narrows.

After the First World War the ships of the company were in turn taken over by Furness, Withy, who elected to pour money into the tourist development of Bermuda. In 1920 they built the Bermudiana Hotel as the first step in their Bermuda expansion. They went on to create the Mid-Ocean Club at Tucker's Town, which remains a fashionable area, and the Castle Harbour Hotel. In 1958 the Bermudiana, then under the ownership of Sir Harold Wernher, burnt down, but was rebuilt (and in 1998 it is being taken down to be replaced by offices). The Castle Harbour has been renovated on several occasions, most recently by the present leaseholders, the Marriott Hotel chain, whose work on the building has included con-siderable expansion, so that it remains one of Bermuda's finest hotels.

These improvements met opposition, particularly in the case of the Mid-Ocean Club. Although Tucker's Town was sparsely popu-lated, some of the people who lived there objected to selling and being forced to move out. Furness, Withy were backed, however, by an act of the Legislature under which properties could be acquired whether the owners liked it or not. Many Bermudians of both races objected to this situation, but the land was taken and the Mid-Ocean Club was born. It proved to be a boon to some of the inhab-itants, for it was immediately popular with well-to-do Americans, and created many jobs and an improved standard of living for those who had survived previously on crops from smallholdings and fishing. The importance of the development of Tourism may be judged by the decline of the agricultural industry. For instance, in 1919 Bermuda exported 91 777 barrels of potatoes, but by 1925 this had declined to 23 448. The export of Bermuda onions suffered even more, dropping from 153 000 crates in 1914 to 21 570 in 1925. In 1930 harsh increases in US Customs Duties almost stopped Bermuda's agricultural exports.

Bermuda was also faced with the problem of supporting a rapidly increasing population. There were about 17 000 people living here in 1900, but this rose to 20 127 in 1921 and 27 789 in 1931. At the same time British interest in the Bermuda base waned. In 1907 just over 1300 troops were stationed in Bermuda; from 1920 to 1939 the strength was about 700. In 1914 just over 1000 men were carried on the books at the Dockyard; but in 1919 this was reduced to 400.

These circumstances meant that, despite the hardships caused by the building of the Mid-Ocean Club, the money Furness, Withy poured into Bermuda and the subsequent rise in numbers of visitors was extremely important to the community. Some idea of the growth of the tourist trade is shown in figures for tourist arrivals (see Table 2 below).

A Notable Resident

One quiet but notable person who came to Bermuda with his Bermudian wife to live was Professor Reginald Aubrey Fessenden. Professor Fessenden was an inventor, and his major invention was voice radio. It was Guglielmo Marconi who first used Hertzian waves to transmit morse code over the air, but his wireless theory and methods brought him to a dead end. Fessenden thought up the correct method and managed to prove it in a laboratory at the University of Pittsburgh, and in 1900 followed up with transmissions over a mile.

In 1906 he managed to send and receive voice messages across the Atlantic from the town of Brant Rock, near Plymouth in Massachusetts, but then the radio tower in Scotland blew down in a storm and he was not able to prove what had occurred. That Christmas, however, he transmitted the first radio broadcast to ships at sea, consisting of Christmas readings and carols. For many years Fessenden was cheated of the proper rewards for his inventions. When the final settlement was made in 1928 he and his wife purchased Wistowe in Flatts. He died there in 1931.

Table 2   Visitors to Bermuda in the inter-war period

Year	No. of stay-over visitors	No. of cruise ship visitors
1920	13 327	–
1930	46 463	7 668
1937	58 646	24 169

No Cars!

Bermudians decided to continue doing without cars, in part because the tourists of the time enjoyed a place that had no autos. At the turn of the century motor cars had been playthings for the rich, but when Henry Ford started manufacturing his Model T car on an assembly-line basis and sold it at prices which were within the reach of most Americans, the picture changed, and the car rapidly became the most important means of transportation. At first this was welcomed because cars were cleaner than horses, but as they grew in numbers they brought troubles in their wake, and many Americans were glad to escape them for a holiday. Bermuda therefore became a motorless Eden. Even the British Army and the Royal Navy continued to use horse-drawn transport on Bermuda roads right up to the early days of the Second World War. In the late 1930s Bermuda's stand on motorisation was to lead to an odd incident when the Legislature turned down a request by Governor Sir Reginald Hildyard for a car; the Governor, enraged, resigned.

Means of Transportation

In the earliest days Bermudians had travelled about the islands principally by boat, so that when Norwood made his survey he arranged for there to be rights of way from shore to shore every two shares. These came to be called tribe roads, some of which still exist. The tribe roads were narrow; it seems likely that they were designed to be wide enough to roll a barrel, a system of transporting freight which appears to have existed for a considerable time. A road was opened from one end of the island to the other, again apparently of barrel width, and this appears to have gone along the tops of the hills. Perhaps it was a throwback to England where hilltops were best as a safeguard against mud and snowdrifts, or perhaps it was felt that this was a way of keeping a lookout for ships, whether friends or enemies.

As noted earlier, in the 19th century the British Army built the South Shore Road from Tucker's Town to Southampton so that they could take troops and guns rapidly to any beach threatened by an enemy landing party. Much of the road runs behind the hills to give troops protection from ship's guns and to hide their movement.

During the 19th century a system of horse buses linked Somerset and St George's with Hamilton. They carried both freight and passengers, and stopped anywhere along the road to pick up or put down passengers. A trip on one of these buses could be quite an adventure. Sometimes everyone had to jump out and chase a chicken which had escaped from its cage. And of course people also walked from one place to another, as they must have done from the start of the colony.

At the end of the 19th century the modern safety bicycle came into existence, and Bermudians took to two wheels with great joy. The bicycles were faster than a horse, cheaper to look after, and an excellent way of travelling five miles or more. The ferries – the first steam ferry was introduced in 1867 – readily took bicycles for a small extra payment, as did the Bermuda Railway, which was built in the late 1920s and early 1930s to provide faster transportation for Bermuda while keeping out motor cars.

The idea of the railway faced opposition, particularly from the owners of livery stables, but the government decided to encourage the scheme of building a narrow gauge railway from Somerset to St George's. A company was formed in England and was given powers to purchase land compulsorily, and in 1931 the first trains started running. In many places the train trip gave breathtaking views, and the line had a strong appeal for visitors. Bermudians made good use of it, too, but the cost of punching the line through the hills and bridging the valleys proved enormously expensive, and the company did not pay.

Liners

Apart from hotel building, Furness, Withy spent money to develop the New York–Bermuda steamship run. Their first new ship was the *Bermuda*, but soon after she started she had the misfortune to catch fire alongside in Hamilton. The small Hamilton Fire Brigade fought the fire as well as they could, but the ship's seacocks had to be opened and she was sunk alongside. Furness, however, had already started building the *Monarch of Bermuda*, a splendid passenger liner containing all the most modern refinements of the time. They followed her with a sister ship, the *Queen of Bermuda*, and these two ships set new standards on the New York–Bermuda run. Both

*The Bermuda Railway: the trains used to travel down
the middle of Front Street*

vessels had sufficient freight capacity, including a cattle deck, for most of Bermuda's imports from the United States. Another fine group of liners which visited Bermuda were the 'Lady' liners of Canadian National Steamships, which ran from Canada to Bermuda and the West Indies.

In 1938 a new rival appeared on the scene when Pan American Airways and Imperial Airways started a joint American-British airline service between Bermuda and Long Island. Pan American flew the *Betsy*, a Sikorsky S42 flying boat, while Imperial Airways, which later became part of the British Overseas Airways Corporation (now British Airways), had the *Cavalier*, one of a splendid series of Empire Class flying boats. It was a design which gained fame during the Second World War as the Sunderland.

Unfortunately the motors of the Empire flying boats had not been properly equipped to face icy weather, and as winter came on there were occasional problems as the carburettors iced up and failed to provide fuel to one engine or another. This could usually be

The Betsy

The Cavalier

**The two flying boats which inaugurated the scheduled
air service between New York and Bermuda**

cleared by making the engine backfire, but on the evening of 21 January 1939 this expedient failed, and the flying boat with her 13 passengers and crew was forced down on the water. As soon as she hit she started to sink, but most of the passengers and crew managed to escape. Fortunately the crew had managed to radio a distress signal before the *Cavalier* crashed, and the aircraft herself had reached the Gulf Stream, so that the water was not freezing cold.

Ships started searching immediately, but it was eleven hours before the sweeping searchlight of the tanker *Esso Baytown* discovered the little huddle of ten survivors in the water and brought them aboard. One of those who perished was Robert Spence, a steward, who died eight hours after the crash having gallantly spent his energy helping others.

One of the survivors was Mrs Edna Watson, who later became one of Bermuda's two first women MCPs (the other was Mrs R.D. Aitken). Up to the time of writing (1997) that has been the only crash on the New York–Bermuda run.

The Water Supply

A notable accomplishment of the inter-war years was the first successful attack on the chronic problem of Bermuda's water supply. When ships were wrecked on Bermuda before the first settlement, the hardest task their crews faced was finding fresh water. Some might be discovered in shallow depressions in the rocks, and wells might produce fresh water or salt. The first settlers must have discovered early on that water from the frequent rain could be stored in barrels or tanks such as exist today. They found nearly fresh water in the marshes and used it for cattle, and they dug wells, usually by the seashore, which worked all right except in times of drought. Periods of drought remained an enormous problem. Tanks went dry as the water was used up, and the marsh and well water became steadily more salt-laden.

The great accomplishment of the period was made by Sir Harry Watlington. He felt that if the fresh water floating on the salt in Devonshire Marsh could be tapped through the use of horizontal channels cut into the marsh, it could be purified and pumped into a big tank and then fed into Hamilton for washing and flushing. He invested a great deal of money in the plan, and it worked. Water was provided for Hamilton, and later for Paget and further west, providing Bermuda's first water system. Since then more horizontal wells have been driven into the hillsides around the marsh, and new purification systems mean that the supply is now safe for drinking. Salt water is being made potable by the same system.

When the Bermuda government purchased the imperial lands at Prospect they obtained an enormous tank built by the Army in the moat of Fort Prospect. This was used for some years in conjunction with a distillation plant to provide drinkable water, and other distillation plants were installed by hotels. Since then the government and private persons have taken advantage of the great lenses of water which were first discovered by a man with a dowsing rod. The American writer Kenneth Roberts, who had a house in Bermuda, had great faith in a man named Henry Gross, and brought him to Bermuda when the island was suffering from a severe drought. Gross used his dowsing rod to discover places where deep wells might be sunk. The wells produced an abundant supply of fresh water, and so the fresh water lenses were discovered. The abundant supply of water has led Bermudians to use more and more water, many people being prepared to purchase it rather than following their forefathers in using it sparingly.

SOURCES
Fessenden, *Fessenden, Builder of Tomorrows*.
Stuart *et al.* (eds) *Bermuda's Delicate Balance*.
Raby, *Radio's First Voice*.
Roberts, *Henry Gross and his Dowsing Rod*.
Zuill, W.E.S., *Bermuda Journey* (1st edition).

18

War and American Bases

During the 1930s Germany, defeated in the First World War, fell under the spell of the brutal, amoral and remarkable demagogue Adolf Hitler. He revived the armaments industry, developed a powerful army and air force and began rebuilding the German navy. He gave Germans a sense of pride after the defeat of 1918 and what many considered the cruel terms of the Treaty of Versailles. Germany rapidly became a threat to world peace as he merged Austria with Germany, obtained the Sudetenland of Czechoslovakia and then the rest of the country, and a few months later menaced Poland. The British Empire went to war on 3 September 1939, three days after Poland was invaded. The invasion was highly successful, the *coup de grace* coming when Russia attacked from the east and took a portion of the country.

With Poland finished as a nation Britain and France found themselves allied against Germany, but for many months the enemies faced one another across the Franco-German border and little else occurred – a period known as the 'phoney war'. For Bermuda the war almost immediately endangered the tourist trade, with both the *Queen* and the *Monarch* being required for military service, the *Queen* as an armed merchant cruiser and the *Monarch* as a troop transport. Even before they were taken off the New York–Bermuda run travelling on them became uncomfortable, since the portholes had to be kept sealed in case the ships were hit by a torpedo, and no lights could be shown on deck at night. In any case, travellers seeking a relaxing holiday were not likely to travel on belligerent ships nor visit an island at war.

Although the British garrison was enlarged and Bermudians were recruited into the local forces, which went on a full-time basis, with tourism so badly affected the economy faltered. Public works were increased and the Bermuda Labour Corps was formed, providing employment but at low rates of pay. The main accomplishment of the corps still stands today, for the workers built Bernard Park (named after the Governor, Sir Denis Bernard) and Dutton Avenue running through it (named after the Colonial Secretary of the time).

At sea, as in the First World War, events involved ships and men Bermuda knew. In 1937 Commodore Henry Harwood, in charge of the Southern Division of the America and West Indies Squadron, visited Bermuda in HMS *Exeter* for exercises and conferences with the Commander-in-Chief of the station.

The Battle of the River Plate

Two years later this same commander and his ship were to play the principal role in the Battle of the River Plate, which led to the destruction of the German pocket battleship *Admiral Graf Spee*. The German pocket battleships with their 11-inch guns were designed to outfight any ships they could not escape from, and to be self-contained commerce raiders like the privateers of the past. The discovery soon after the outbreak of the war that two of these ships had already sailed from Germany led to a considerable fear among the authorities in Bermuda, for it was realized that either of them could approach the South Shore in the vicinity of Warwick and Southampton and shell the Dockyard without a single gun being able to reply. With difficulty a spare six-inch gun barrel at St David's battery was taken to Warwick Camp, put in working order, and mounted there in the hope that such an attack could at least be discouraged. The gun was never needed, but that was only one example of the difficulties the French and British faced in combating the pocket battleship menace. Heavy ships were deployed all over the Atlantic in hunting groups, causing a diversion of effort.

Smallest of the groups was Commodore Harwood's Force G, stationed off the River Plate. On 13 December the *Graf Spee* appeared over the horizon, and Commodore Harwood started firing as soon as she came within range. His ships were the *Exeter*, with eight-inch guns, and the six-inch cruisers *Ajax* and *Achilles* – the *Achilles* was part of the Royal New Zealand Navy. In little over an hour the *Exeter* had been nearly destroyed, but the *Graf Spee* had also suffered damage. The two light cruisers were faster and as she could not shake them off she ran into the Uruguayan port of Montevideo. She emerged 72 hours later, but before she reached the waiting British ships Captain Hans Langsdorf ordered her blown up. Two days later he shot himself, leaving behind a note which said in part: 'I am happy to pay with my life for any possible reflection on the honour of the flag.'

German Victories

Early in 1940 Germany started on a series of startling victories. First Denmark and Norway fell to the German forces, then Holland, Belgium, Luxembourg and finally France herself. Italy declared war on Germany's side. Britain therefore faced a Europe united under a conqueror. During this time Bermudians had worked hard to try and maintain the tourist trade and succeeded in persuading the American President Lines to run ships here. It was a magnificent effort, but American travellers were not interested.

In May 1940 a contingent of the Bermuda Volunteer Rifle Corps sailed for England, and during the summer large naval convoys gathered here. Many of the ships needed repairs and the unemployment situation was eased. One tragedy of the year was the gallant fight of HMS *Jervis Bay*. The *Jervis Bay* was not a warship at all. Like the *Queen of Bermuda* she was a liner which had been pressed into service to help patrol the sea lanes and to do odd jobs which required vessels which could carry six-inch guns. She had been a frequent visitor here as a convoy escort.

On 5 November 1940 the ship was north of Bermuda escorting a convoy bound for England when suddenly the German pocket battleship *Scheer* loomed over the horizon. Although his ship was completely outclassed, Captain E. S. F Fegen decided to attack the *Scheer* in the hope of delaying her so that the ships of the convoy could scatter and escape. Captain Fegen was successful, and although his ship was soon badly damaged, he continued to point her at the raider as long as she could steer and move. Finally the *Jervis Bay* sank, but the ships of the convoy managed to scatter and many of them succeeded in getting away. Her crew had many friends in Bermuda and a memorial was erected at Albuoy's Point.

Censorship

By November 1940 many changes had occurred in Bermuda. The first one came as a result of Britain's decision to intercept mails from the United States bound for Europe. By this time Pan American Airways was flying the only civilian air route across the North Atlantic with Boeing 314 flying boats touching down at Bermuda and the Azores before reaching Lisbon. Mail was taken off and ships were herded into port to remove surface mail and contraband goods bound for enemy destinations.

Censorship required large numbers of expert linguists, and soon the Princess and Bermudiana Hotels were in full swing again, the Princess as censorship headquarters, and the Bermudiana as sleeping quarters for the censors. The work of the censors led to the discovery of several German spies in the United States, and information was quietly passed to the American authorities.

A Boeing 314 Pan American clipper

In one notable success 270 famous impressionist paintings were taken off the American Export Lines ship *Excalibur* in Hamilton. They were being taken from France to New York, where the British were sure they would be sold to provide much needed American dollars for Hitler. The paintings, known as the Vollard Collection, were in the strongroom of the liner, and the captain refused to open the door. The British security officer, Mr H. Montgomery Hyde, ordered the door opened with an oxyacetylene flame burner, and removed the paintings. They were stored for a time in the vaults of the Bank of Bermuda, and later sent to Canada where they were kept for the duration of the war in the Canadian National Gallery.

American Bases

But the big change for Bermuda came when Winston Churchill, the strong, pugnacious, energetic and defiant Prime Minister of Britain, and President Franklin D. Roosevelt of the United States agreed, on 3 September 1940, exactly a year after Britain entered the war, that the United States should acquire, on 99-year leases, bases in Bermuda, Newfoundland, the Bahamas, Jamaica, Antigua, St Lucia, Trinidad and British Guiana. The Bermuda and Newfoundland bases were given to the United States; the others were in exchange for fifty old destroyers of the US Navy, desperately needed for the anti-submarine battle. The scheme was accepted in the United States as being a good business deal of great benefit to the country. From the other side, although the Royal Navy considered the destroyers of rather dubious value, the deal meant that the United States would be committed to the defence of the areas where the bases were situated and was thus drawn closer to coming into the war on the British side.

Soon after the deal was announced a US survey team arrived on the cruiser USS *St Louis* to look for a site for the base. The main problem was to find a place for an airfield on hilly Bermuda, and one where a runway could be built facing south-west, in the direction of the most frequent winds. Heavily laden airplanes of the 1940s needed to take off into the wind. At first the Americans thought of thrusting an airfield through the Warwick hills from sea to sea, cutting Bermuda in half, but this scheme was superseded by another after Commander Guy Ridgway, a Royal Navy officer who had made his home in Bermuda and was serving on the staff of the British Admiral, revived the idea of Mr B.V.S. Smith of using Castle Harbour, where a line of reefs ran out in a south-westerly direction. His idea was to fill in the area between the reefs and the shore, which he suggested would be an easier task and would still enable Bermudians to travel by land from one end of the island to the other.

The Americans agreed, but decided that the base would require a large slice of St David's Island as well as all of Cooper's Island and Long Bird Island and a number of smaller islands as well. They also wanted to site a naval base in the Great Sound at Morgan's and Tucker's Islands, where they had a base during the First World War. In fact even before the Churchill-Roosevelt agreement there had been discussions about an American seaplane base in the Great Sound. The amount of land required from a small country was enormous, and Bermudians tried to point this out to their British and American friends by estimating what the loss of one-eighth of the British Isles or the continental United States would entail. Nevertheless, with Britain up against the wall, without allies, facing a powerful and successful Germany, there was considerable fear that the island nation would succumb, and the Americans hastened to secure their new holdings. In Bermuda troops poured in and construction was carried out with great speed. Hills fell before bulldozers, sand poured ashore from big dredgers, the shoreline disappeared, houses and trees were smashed and destroyed. It was construction on a scale Bermuda had never seen before, and has not seen since.

Homes had to be found for the people of St David's Island, and the Bermuda Government launched a house-building programme in an area called Texas, just outside the base. There had been a plan for using Smith's Island, but that ended when the islanders made it plain they wanted to stay on St David's.

And so the airfield was built. Bermudians went to work for the American contractors at lower rates of pay than the Americans. This was in accordance with the Base Agreement, the idea being to try not to upset the Bermuda economy. This situation led to the eventual founding of trade unions here (see Chapter 21). Despite problems, many people prospered through this work, saved their money and helped lay the groundwork for the prospering island

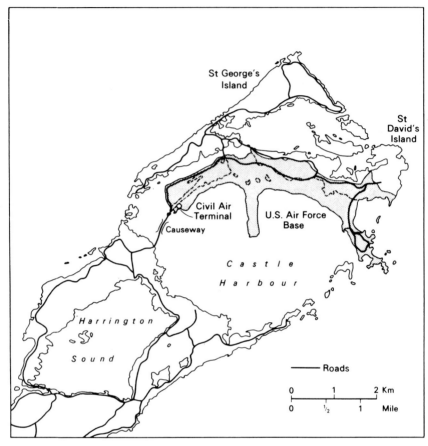

The area of the island covered by the US base

of the second half of the 20th century. With hordes of American soldiers and sailors and contractors' personnel on Bermuda the depressed wartime economy changed radically. Goods and services were at a premium, and it was generally felt that Bermuda came out of the war richer than it went into it.

Relationships with the Americans were, at first, not happy. The dignified tourist resort of pre-war days rapidly changed character under the impact of hundreds of young men, and many Bermudians were bewildered by it. Others made high profits out of the situation. In addition, the needs of war required an end to some of the anti-motorization laws, and soon military vehicles were speeding up and down the roads, frightening horses and changing the entire tempo of Bermudian life. But on 7 December 1941, the Japanese made a surprise attack on Pearl Harbour, the US Navy's main base in the Pacific, and America went to war with the Japanese. Soon after the Germans and Italians declared war on the US, and America was fully embroiled in the global conflict. This made an immediate difference in Bermudian attitudes to the Americans, and from then on there was far more cooperation as the British, American and Canadian forces stationed here worked together to win the war.

Churchill's Visit

Soon after Pearl Harbour Mr Churchill made a trip to the United States and Canada, and then took a brief holiday in Florida. On 14 January 1942 he boarded one of the big Boeing 314 flying boats at Hampton Roads and flew in beautiful weather to Bermuda. Here he was planning to board the battleship *Duke of York* for the trip to England.

On the afternoon of his arrival Mr Churchill addressed the House of Assembly. He writes about it in his book *The Grand Alliance*:

> ... I addressed the Bermuda Assembly, which is the oldest Parliamentary institution in the Western Hemisphere. I pleaded with them to give their assent and all their aid to the establishment of the United States naval and air bases in the island, about which they were in some distress. The life of the whole Empire was at stake. The smooth working of our alliance with the United States made victory certain, no matter how long the road might be. They did not demur.

The flight to Bermuda had gone well, and the Prime Minister was anxious to be back in London. So he decided to fly back direct from Bermuda all the way in the flying boat. It was a daring plan in wartime, with the uncertainties of weather and enemy aircraft, and indeed at one point the flying boat lost its way and nearly flew over German-occupied Brest. But the plan succeeded, and Mr Churchill returned safely to Britain to continue running the Empire until the end of the war.

German Submarines

One result of the American entry into the war nearly brought disaster. Up to this time German submarines had operated mainly in the eastern and central Atlantic, attacking the stubbornly defended convoys bringing vital food and raw materials to Britain from the rest of the world. Now, however, Admiral Doenitz, the able German officer in charge of submarines, decided that the Americans were probably unprepared for war, so he shifted his attack to the American coast and Atlantic seaboard. It was a successful move, and ship after ship was sunk.

Off Bermuda one vessel packed with food supplies for humans and animals fell victim to a submarine, and during the middle of 1942 Bermuda went on very short rations. The situation was only saved when an American convoy arrived: the ships were cheered as they came into port. But it was too late to save many of the horses, and private persons mourned their family pets, while carters, farmers and livery stable owners saw their sources of income disappearing. It was a tragic occurrence which made it easier to introduce motorisation after the war.

Wartime shipping had become haphazard, with calls for freighters in so many areas of the world, but as the submarine menace was conquered, and as the production of ships from American shipyards enabled the allies to replace the vessels which had been sunk, the little Norwegian freighter *Braga* was placed on the run to the United States.

A frequent visitor to Bermuda which came to a tragic end was the French submarine *Surcouf*, the largest submarine in the world at the outbreak of war. She even carried an aircraft. The *Surcouf* became part of the Free French forces – composed of those Frenchmen who continued fighting Germany when France was defeated – and for a period the big submarine was stationed here. Her end came on 18 February 1942, when she disappeared. It is believed that she sunk after a collision with an American merchant vessel in the Gulf of Mexico, but there have been many rumours about her fate, including suggestions that she was secretly sinking allied ships and, after this was discovered, was sunk by allied forces.

Another unexpected visitor came to Bermuda in 1944 and stayed here. It was one of the best kept secrets of the war when the

German submarine U-505 was captured off Cape Verde by an American task force commanded by Captain Daniel V. Gallery. Captain Gallery had had a chance of capturing another U-boat previously, but his men were unprepared and the submarine sank before she could be boarded. This time he was ready, and when his carrier sub-hunting force attacked U-505 and brought her to the surface, Commander Hall of the USS *Pillsbury* sent away a boarding party in a whaleboat. The US sailors clambered aboard the slowly sinking German submarine, managed to disconnect the demolition charges, and, with the help of extra pumps from the US ships, stopped her from going down. On 19 June 1944 the U-boat arrived here under tow. Later she was used as a 'tame' submarine in the training of allied anti-submarine squadrons. Not even her own sailors (who had been captured and sent below decks immediately after they abandoned the U-boat) knew that she had been saved, so that the allies learned much about the German Navy and its codes without any Germans being aware of it.

Bermuda Troops

As they had in the First World War, many Bermudians served abroad. A contingent of the BVRC joined the Lincolnshire Regiment as they had before, but this time the BMA and its wartime offspring, the Bermuda Militia Infantry, became part of the Caribbean Regiment. The BVRC saw service in France, while the Caribbean Regiment was in the Middle East. Altogether 184 Bermudians served abroad in this way: 37 died and one was reported missing.

A number of Bermudians joined the Royal Air Force and the Royal Canadian Air Force, thanks to a flying school which was started soon after the outbreak of war. They served in many theatres of war, and had many different adventures. The war ended on 8 May 1945 in Europe and 2 September 1945 in the Pacific.

Wartime Life

Compared to many other countries Bermuda scarcely suffered during the Second World War, but there were hazards and shortages which made life more difficult, particularly after the U-boat offensive started in 1942. Some strange solutions were found to problems, such as the introduction of a sailing ship service from the West Indies. There was the summer when bread was rationed and authorities only allowed the sale of day-old bread on the theory that it would be less palatable and people would eat less. The trouble was that the flour scraped from the bottom of the bins was not very good, and the day-old bread would often have mould running right through it.

Shoes were rationed, as was powdered milk, butter and sugar. Rubber tyres were in short supply, and the roads went from bad to worse as the big American and British trucks and tanks rolled over them, creating large potholes. Some people used large ropes around the rims of their pedal cycle wheels, and carriage drivers cut up used truck tyres to keep their carriages rolling.

Probably the best food in the island was to be found at the American bases, and pet dogs ran off to rifle the soldiers' and sailors' garbage cans. People were encouraged to plant as much food as possible, and a canning factory was started to preserve Bermuda vegetables. Some people even attempted to make soap, which also was hard to get.

It was not an entirely gloomy time. War produces worries and sorrows, but it also produces a feeling of togetherness which is inspiring and helps to offset the melancholy side, an aspect of human nature which seems to go alongside the devastation and horror of war.

War song

A Bermuda song of the war was 'Mr Trimingham and Mr Trott' sung to the tune of an American song, 'Mr Gallagher and Mr Shean'. It was written, according to the late Mrs John Knowlton, on the verandah of her house in Paget, 'Sanctuary', by two young American Navy officers who thought up the lines and tossed them back and forth. The mockery of the song was sufficient to amuse Bermudians as well, and more verses were added by local singers, notably the Talbot Brothers. Here are some of the verses:

> Oh Mr Trimingham, oh Mr Trimingham
> These Yankees are a blooming lot of bores.
> We have tried all we know to relieve them of their dough,
> But the blighters still keep coming back for more.

Oh Mr Trott, oh Mr Trott,
We bes' not take all that they got.
If we strip them to the peel, there'll be nothing left to steal!
Absolutely Mr Trimingham! Positively Mr Trott!

Oh Mr Trimingham, oh Mr Trimingham,
What's the matter with these Yankees anyway?
We have given them no land, so they sucked up tons of sand,
And have added many acres to our shores.
Oh Mr Trott, oh Mr Trott,
Now peace will put those Yankees on the spot.
We will charge a goodly fee to replace it in the sea,
And they'll pay it Mr Trimingham? Need I say it Mr Trott!

Oh Mr Trimingham, oh Mr Trimingham,
These Americans are a blooming lot of bores.
In my Inverurie House, someone burnt my chair, the louse,
And the Navy says you can't sue Uncle Sam.
Oh Mr Trott, oh Mr Trott,
Can't you see the great big opportunity you got?
For that chair of which you speak may be sold as an antique.
Where's my buyer Mr Trimingham? At your Belmont,
    Mr Trott.

SOURCES
Block, *Kindley Air Force Base, Bermuda – The First 25 Years.*
Churchill, *The Second World War*, Vol. III.
Hyde, *The Quiet Canadian.*
Tatem, *US Naval Station, Bermuda, 1941–1968.*
Zuill, W.E.S., *Bermuda Journey* (1st edition).

PART 4

Modern Bermuda

19

Half a Century of Change and Stability

As we approach the second millennium of the modern era Bermuda can look back on 50 years of momentous change during which the community has held together, and built a remarkably prosperous lifestyle which has made it quite different from all the other isolated islands in the oceans of the world. The majority of Bermudians took a pragmatic approach to life, as was demonstrated when voters voted against Bermuda's seeking independence from Britain. The question of the costs and benefits of independence dominated the public debate, which bemused more than one outside observer accustomed to emotional rhetoric about 'becoming grown-up' and 'being free' – arguments which were also used in Bermuda.

This chapter furnishes an outline of events while subsequent chapters will tell in more detail about aspects of the change. It was a time when the population soared from 30 000 people in 1939 to 53 000 in 1970 and 60 000 in 1991. This meant that homebuilding had to proceed at an enormous pace to keep up with the increasing numbers of people, to the extent that during the 25 years after the Second World War there was probably more building than during the entire preceding 350 years. During the succeeding 25 years Bermudians started living in blocks of apartments – often on an ownership (condominium) basis: a change from the 'house on a lot of land' which had been the desired norm before.

The face of Bermuda changed, and instead of becoming a land of two municipalities, a few villages, and countryside between, it became a land of two municipalities with suburbs covering the rest of the island, aside from a few green areas: nature reserves and parks, golf courses, and a few privately owned tracts.

At first the need to find employment for the increasing numbers of people led to the building of new hotels, and the requirements of travellers accustomed to up-to-date comforts like air conditioning led to constant improvement of the old hotels. In Bermuda the hotels were the equivalent of factories in other localities, giving employment and bringing money into the community, and from the end of the Second World War onward the tourist business was pushed hard to make up for the rapid post-war rundown of the American bases. Even so, it was not until 1950 that Bermuda topped the 1937 tourist business peak with 61 611 visitors. In 1959 there were 142 330 tourists and only 12 years later, in 1971, Bermuda passed the 400 000 mark with 412 947 visitors.

The tourist business was approaching a new peak of success in 1981 when a long strike by hospital workers brought out many other union divisions in sympathy, including the hotel workers (see Chapter 21). It seemed symbolic of an end to Bermuda's long honeymoon with the tourist business, but in fact figures continued to climb, reaching a peak in 1987 when numbers of tourists reached 637 314. Since then there has been a decline. By 1988 two major hotels had closed down and a third had reduced the number of its rooms, and by 1994 visitor figures had dropped to 590 000. In fact the economic base of the island was changing, symbolized by the decision to rebuild the Bermudiana Hotel, closed since 1988, as offices. This had a particular meaning as the Bermudiana was the first of the Furness, Withy hotels after the First World War.

Exempt Companies

Quietly at first and later with greater public knowledge Bermuda developed a new business. Although it had its origins in the 1930s it really started to gain importance in the 1950s. This new way of making money and keeping the economy afloat was the offshore company business. The companies – which were not allowed to trade within the island – were exempt from many Bermuda regulations, particularly as to ownership, and were therefore known as exempted companies.

The success of these undertakings was a reflection of the increased social conscience of many nations which led to increased taxation and regulation. This was true of both Britain and the United States, and it was from these two countries that Bermuda drew its first customers. Legal minds discovered that there were advantages in setting up companies in such places as Bermuda and the Bahamas, where direct taxes were slight and regulations easier.

While many of these companies exist on paper only, others have large offices and employ many Bermudians, and all contribute to the banking, accounting and legal sectors of the economy. By 1985 an estimated 30 per cent of all economic activity in Bermuda was generated by exempted companies, and in 1992 outside income from international business became higher than income from tourism for the first time. In 1994 the Bermuda Monetary Authority estimated that international business brought in US $401 million while tourism produced US $383 million.

Parallel with the growth of the exempted company business an attempt was made to establish light industry at the old Dockyard. The Royal Navy stopped using Bermuda for ship repairs in 1951, (although a small naval base was retained until 1995) and soon afterwards the British Army was withdrawn. After long negotiations the Bermuda government purchased most of the imperial lands which had been used for military and naval purposes and planned to develop the Dockyard as a free port and factory area.

This scheme was not particularly successful, but in 1974 the Bermuda National Trust persuaded the government that the Keep of the Dockyard, the fortified area where ordnance stores had been kept, could be turned into a Maritime Museum at no expense to the government. A group of Trust members undertook the task and were completely successful. The increased interest in the Dockyard led to the government deciding to turn it into a tourist attraction, and the West End Development Corporation, a government corporation run by an appointed board of directors, was set up to run Boaz, Watford and Ireland Islands. Many problems were overcome and today Ireland Island is a thriving shopping and marine business centre, a pleasant housing estate has risen on Boaz

Island and the green parts of Ireland Island remain an ecological oasis.

The imperial lands at Prospect and St George's were put to different uses, for schools, housing and, at Prospect, for the relocation of Police headquarters, which had been at Hamilton.

Motorization

Today the motor car is taken for granted in Bermuda and the Bermuda way of life is dependent on this form of transport. This makes it difficult to visualize the earlier way of life when goods were carried in horse-drawn carts and carriages were the only means of transportation besides the ubiquitous pedal cycle, and the countryside was peppered with small grocery and variety stores, especially the two competing chains of O. R. Loblein and the A-One.

The idea of shifting over to motor cars was regarded by many people with distaste and distrust, fear of its effect on the slowly developing post-war tourist trade, and the knowledge that the roads, thanks to military vehicles and doctors' cars, were not as safe as they had been. On the other hand Bermuda had lost many of its horses as a result of the feed shortage of 1942, and there could be no doubt that motor vehicles were more comfortable to use than pedal cycles and far more efficient and cleaner than horse-drawn vehicles. Flies breed in dung and flies were a constant problem in the island, impossible to exclude from the home, garden or the grocery store. Then there was the question of numbers of vehicles. Carriages and horses were relatively expensive to own and care for so the roads were not clogged. The United States, however, had reached the stage where nearly everyone could afford a motor car, and rush hours, parking problems and other difficulties had arisen. So, in order to keep Bermuda from being swamped with vehicles, the law was framed in such a way that cars would be expensive to purchase and keep up and secondhand vehicles difficult to obtain and a prohibited import.

With these points enshrined in the legislation the law allowing private use of motor cars was passed in 1946, and the face of Bermuda changed. For Bermudians took to motor cars, mopeds, motorcycles and scooters, and the numbers of automobiles on the roads continues to rise, with 49 000 motorized vehicles registered in

Carriages lined up at Hamilton in the days before motorization

1995. Traffic on roads designed for horse-drawn transport sometimes seems to have reached saturation point, but response to
public demand has led to road changes, such as the creation in the
early 1990s of Bermuda's first four-lane stretch of highway leading
into Hamilton from the Foot of the Lane roundabout.

Motorization soon brought into question the wisdom of maintaining the Bermuda Railway, which was in need of considerable
repair work after being neglected during the war. The decision was
made to dispose of it, and the tracks and rolling stock were sold to
British Guiana (now Guyana). There have been many schemes for
re-establishing some form of light railway, but none have ever
reached fruition. The right of way itself has been turned into a
walking path – the Railway Trail – available for quiet recreation,
and the spectacular views for which the old railway was noted are
still there to be enjoyed.

Not only transport in Bermuda but also transport to Bermuda
changed. In 1938 the flying boats *Cavalier* and the *Betsy* had
given the first air service between Bermuda and New York. Soon
after the *Cavalier* disaster Pan American Airways brought the big,
rugged Boeing 314 flying boats onto the run, and extended the
route across the Atlantic to the Azores and Lisbon. During the war
these aircraft became the only means of travel to America for most
Bermudians.

The war itself brought tremendous improvements in aircraft,
and military necessity led to the development of a network of
airfields and air routes around the world. Land planes superseded
the slower flying boats, and soon after the end of the war the first
airliners started landing at Kindley Air Force Base on daily sched-
ules. The popularity of aircraft increased to the point where they
superseded ships as a means of travelling to Bermuda, particularly
when air fares became cheaper than ship tickets.

Ships were not finished, however. Immediately after the war
Furness, Withy put the small liners *Fort Amherst* and *Fort
Townshend* on the route while they refurbished the *Monarch of
Bermuda*. The *Monarch*, unfortunately, caught fire in the shipyard
when she was nearly ready, and, although the fire was extinguished,
the company decided to sell her, and set to work putting the *Queen
of Bermuda* to rights instead. Eventually the *Queen* was ready, and,
to the great delight of Bermudians, came back on the run. She

continued to give good service year after year, but in the late 1960s age caught up with her, and she was sent to the breakers' yard. It was a sad and sentimental moment for Bermudians when the great ship steamed away for the last time.

During the *Queen*'s last years the role of passenger shipping changed. It turned out that fewer and fewer people wanted to travel by ship just to get to Bermuda, but numbers did want to make a six-day voyage to Bermuda and back again, using the ship as a hotel here. The pattern continues to the present day, and during the spring, summer and autumn tourist season many ships lie alongside the Dockyard, Hamilton and St George's, but no passenger liners call during the winter. At the end of the century cruising is big business in several parts of the globe, but Bermuda remains a premier destination, and the cruise passengers are an important part of the tourist business.

Life and Demise of the Bases

In 1995 all outside military and naval forces withdrew from Bermuda, and for the first time since the beginning of the American Revolutionary War Bermuda found herself without the presence of military personnel apart from her own. The bases had lived a chequered existence after the end of the Second World War, their use varying with the exigencies of the long Cold War and changing developments in military weapons and aircraft.

During the Second World War three powers – Britain, Canada and the United States – had forces in Bermuda. The US services had separate bases, with the Navy based on the US Naval Air Station at Great Sound and the Army at Fort Bell and the Army Air Corps at Kindley Airfield, both on the leased land at the East End. At the end of the war the Army left, and the base was taken over by the new US Air Force.

In the years that followed both US bases were heavily cut back, and the British decided to abandon the greater part of their land at Boaz, Watford and Ireland Islands, and to remove the army garrison completely. The Canadians withdrew. But world hopes for peace were dashed when Western fears of expansionist plans by Soviet Communism were fed by Stalin's refusal to allow a democratic vote in Poland and his takeover of Czechoslovakia. At the same time the West's wartime Chinese ally, Chiang Kai-Shek and his Kuomintang government, were defeated by Communist forces in China and were forced to flee to Taiwan.

Western apprehension was given full expression by Mr Winston Churchill when in an historic speech at Fulton, Missouri, he said that an Iron Curtain had descended on Europe. There seemed to be much truth in this as civil rights were trampled on and as Russia and its allies remained armed. Then came the Korean War. When Communist North Korea made a surprise assault against South Korea, and bottled up the South Korean Army and two US divisions in a small enclave in the south of the country, President Harry S. Truman decided to respond, and the USA rearmed with great rapidity. To Bermuda's consternation civilian operations were put off Kindley Air Force Base so rapidly that for a time check-in and check-out for airliners was conducted in tents on the site of the present air terminal.

There was a further addition to the base when a Strategic Air Command squadron of refuelling planes moved in. That marked the post-war peak of activity at Kindley. The squadron was disbanded as the Air Force moved over to longer range jet refuellers.

In the 1960s American interest in space exploration was sparked by the Russian success in sending a Sputnik satellite around the earth, and the National Aeronautics and Space Administration was formed. Tracking stations were set up around the world. Bermuda lay on the route chosen for the passage of globe-circling satellites lifting off from Cape Canaveral (now Cape Kennedy), and was an obvious choice for the first down-range tracking station. The Bermuda station continued to play an important role after many of the others were given up, providing support to the Apollo moon landing programme. The tracking station remained in being after the closure of all other base activities, but is due to close in its turn before the year 2000. The NASA station was placed on the Air Force Base as a 'tenant' activity. Then in the mid-1960s another 'tenant' arrived when a US Navy patrol squadron using land aircraft was stationed on Bermuda and took over from the flying boats so long stationed at the Navy base in on Great Sound. A few years later, in 1970, the Air Force withdrew its last squadron and turned the base over to the Navy, which promptly dropped the word 'Kindley'.

The Great Sound Naval Air Station became the 'annex' of the base at the airfield. The varying nomenclature has caused some confusion, so that for many persons the airfield remains 'Kindley' while the old Naval Air Station remained 'NAS'. It was some years before 'the Annex' slowly gained acceptance. Of course at the same time most people still call Ireland Island 'the Dockyard', even though no large ships have been repaired there for 50 years. Now new names are being worked out for the US base lands, which no doubt will confuse matters further.

The Canadians returned to run a wireless tracking station at Daniel's Head, Somerset, and the US Navy set up a submarine listening post at Tudor Hill in Southampton. This was connected to a long range underwater network of cables capable of tracking submarines. At the same time a 'Texas Tower' similar to ones constructed to drill for oil in the sea was set up on the Argus bank and was soon known as Argus Island. It was a useful mark for navigators and withstood all that the Atlantic could throw at it, but eventually it was no longer needed and was dumped in the ocean, making a new home for fish. The long range network made it possible to monitor Soviet nuclear submarines, so that they could be dealt with in the event that the two superpowers decided to go to war and attack one another with nuclear warheads atop rockets launched from submarines. The network is of such value that in 1997 it was being taken over by the Bermuda Biological Station for Research as a tool for studying the lives of whales and other species.

The closest Bermuda came to this naval part of the Cold War was in 1986, when a Soviet missile submarine sank over 600 miles north-east of Bermuda. Surveillance over the area was carried out by Bermuda-based aircraft.

Shipwrecks and the 'Triangle'

Bermuda's northern and western reefs stretch so far out into the sea that Bermuda is often not visible from ships on the edge of them. This has always made them a hazard for mariners since the Spanish first navigated these waters. Therefore Bermudians were not particularly troubled at first when in the decade from 1978 several large vessels grounded on the reefs and were eventually pulled off.

Then came the wreck in 1986 on the north rocks of the supertanker *Aguila Azteca* carrying nearly 200 000 tons of Mexican crude oil. Fortunately the ship was pulled off with little oil spillage, but it was realized that had there been a northerly gale she could have broken up, spilling her cargo in an ecological disaster of enormous consequence to Bermuda, probably forcing the evacuation of most people from the island. Bermuda succeeded in having the waters of the island declared off limits to passing shipping, and built a string of beacons on the reefs, an important and successful change bidding goodbye to the days when a vessel on the reefs was said to be a 'turtle in the net'.

There was a curious sidelight to the grounding of the *Azteca*. The tale is told by a lawyer who went out to the tanker after the enormously valuable vessel grounded. The shore party were on the bridge, and the lawyer, a yachtsman, looked at the ship's chart of the Atlantic. He noticed something odd about it, took it up, and saw light coming through it picking out the mythical Bermuda Triangle.

Under questioning the captain said that he was afraid of the Triangle, and had pencilled it in on his chart. When the tanker grounded he erased his triangle – but the erasure had removed some of the paper, allowing the light to come through. Because he was afraid of the triangle he made each voyage from the Gulf of Mexico to the Straits of Gibraltar north of Bermuda. On this voyage the engine had broken down and had taken 18 hours to repair – so he was late and was trying to shave past Bermuda as close as he could. Thus the *Aguila Azteca* is the only verifiable victim of the Bermuda Triangle.

SOURCES
Block, *Kindley Air Force Base, Bermuda – The First 25 Years*.
Harris, *Bermuda Forts*.
Stuart *et al.* (eds) *Bermuda's Delicate Balance*.
Rushe, *Your Bermuda*.
Stewart, *Bermuda, an Economy which Works*.
Tatem, *US Naval Station, Bermuda, 1941–1968*.

20

Political and Constitutional Change

The 1950s and 1960s were a time of great political change in Bermuda, a period when the traditional ways by which the Bermuda community was governed came to an end. Since then the island has settled into its new form of government and up to 1998 had even, through successive elections, kept the same political party in power. In that year the Progressive Labour Party finally succeeded in ousting the United Bermuda Party from leadership in a powerful showing which gave them 26 seats in the Assembly to the UBP's 14. This followed an unsuccessful effort by members of the UBP in 1995 to lead the island to independence, an idea turned down by the electorate in a referendum.

A major change in Bermuda's way of doing things could have occurred when the Premier of the day, Sir John Swan, tried to lead the island to independence in 1995. The views of Bermudians were ascertained by a referendum, and a strong majority of those who voted were against the idea.

Past Changes

The first major change in Bermuda's constitutional history occurred in 1684 when Charles II dissolved the Bermuda Company and Bermuda became a colony directly under the Crown. The new form of government followed that of most colonies at the time. The Governor had executive power and right to veto laws passed by the Legislature, but he could not force the Legislature to pass laws. Nor could he force them to vote for taxes or agree to spending money for objects with which they disagreed. Laws the Governor accepted might still be vetoed in London, but normally became the law of the land until word of such a veto arrived in the colony.

The Governor ran the executive side of government with the aid of a Governor's Council who were appointed by the British government, although the Governor's recommendations carried a good deal of weight. As well as their executive duties the Council were also the upper house of the legislature, and in the early days of Bermuda's being a royal colony the Council often sat as a court.

The constitution remained this way right up to 1968 with a few small changes. Interestingly enough, many of the basic ideas which developed with this form of constitution were picked up and extended by the new American States, and finally were enshrined in the American constitution. The separation of the executive, representative and judicial functions of the US government made it quite different from the developing British constitution which was already placing executive power in the hands of the elected representatives in the House of Commons.

In Bermuda there was an important change in 1888 when the Council was divided into an Executive Council presided over by the Governor and a Legislative Council presided over by the Chief Justice. The Legislative Council was solely concerned with passing laws, but by tradition was not supposed to interfere with money bills. A coming major change was foreshadowed in 1944 when, after a long campaign in the twenties and thirties, Bermuda women landowners were granted the right to vote.

The preservation of Bermuda's ancient constitution until the late 1960s was quite remarkable. It outlasted the American Revolution, and the period during the 19th century when Britain brought many such constitutions to an end. In view of the importance of the Bermuda base this was particularly striking. In the first decades of the 20th century Bermuda, the Bahamas and Barbados were unique in the Empire for retaining this form of representative government. The three 'Bs' were called 'colonies' in Colonial Office nomenclature – the others, where the Governor's powers were far greater, were called 'Crown colonies'. Barbados first moved toward executive power for the House of Assembly in 1946, and the Bahamas followed in 1964. Bermuda came last. Now Barbados, largest of the three, is independent, and so is the Bahamas, which made the change in 1973. Bermuda remains one of the last remnants of the British Empire, and, surprisingly for so small a place, the most populous outside the British Isles.

Black Representation

Bermuda's franchise also remained unchanged for the greater part of the period. By 1834 those who owned land worth £30 or more could vote, but in that year of Emancipation the Legislature increased the requirement to £60, in what was obviously a move to keep white people in power.

Responding to this situation, black people banded together in political associations. Each parish returned four members to the House of Assembly, and by voting for only one of the four, black voters could make sure of electing their candidate. The practice, known as plumping, was a powerful weapon, and helped to increase the number of black people in the Legislature in the 19th century. Some recent constitutional theorists feel multi-member constituencies have a value in a democracy as a means of giving minorities a better voice in government.

The first black man to become a Member of the Colonial Parliament was Mr William Henry Thomas Joell, a carpenter, who was elected in 1883. Another early black MCP was Mr John Henry T. Jackson, a grocer. These men 'broke down the door' and from then on the Legislature was multi-racial, but Mr Joell and Mr Jackson felt they relied on white voters as well as black ones to become members.

Gradually black representation in the House increased, but it was only in the 1950s that black MCPs were able to make their voices and views strongly felt. That this occurred was due in part to changes in the world outside Bermuda, in part to the influence of the Second World War and the US Bases, but more than any of these to the influence of Dr Edgar Fitzgerald Gordon.

Dr Gordon was elected to the House of Assembly in 1943, having failed to gain a seat many years earlier. In 1944 he accepted the leadership of the Bermuda Workers Association (see next chapter) and had an immediate influence, vastly increasing its membership. The following year Dr Gordon organized a series of meetings in every parish at which he proposed that a petition should be sent to London asking for a Royal Commission to investigate conditions here. He took the petition to London where the Labour Party was in power, and thanks to friends of Mr E.T. Richards, who was studying law in London at the time, was able to meet the Secretary

Dr E.F. Gordon

of State for the Colonies, Mr Arthur Creech Jones – which came as a bad surprise to many Bermudians in positions of leadership.

The petition became the basis for a British government document called Command Paper 7093. It was a tremendous effort, but at the time it fell flat. The Legislature considered the petition and issued a report on it, and that was about all. Changes were still many years away.

Dr Gordon failed in two bids to be re-elected in 1948, but there were crowd scenes at the polls in Southampton and St George's (different parishes had different polling days) which foreshadowed events to come. In 1953 Dr Gordon tried again, and succeeded in being elected, along with eight other black people, the largest black representation in the 36 member House up to that date. Among the MCPs were Mr W.L. Tucker, who was to become the leader in the Legislature of the movement for universal adult suffrage (one vote for every adult), Mr E.T. Richards (later Sir Edward Richards) who in 1972 became government leader, and Mr Walter Robinson, in 1972 Parliamentary Leader of the Progressive Labour Party.

Dr Gordon died in 1955, but he had left an indelible mark on the community. His leadership had at times been rejected, but his drive and showmanship and courage made a strong impact on Bermuda. He not only gave a tremendous impetus to the long battle for racial desegregation, but he also did the same with the trade union movement (see Chapter 21).

The Turning Point of 1959

In the 1958 election his loss was felt when the numbers of black representatives dropped from nine to six, but the following year was an important one in this era of change. It was the 350th anniversary of Sir George Somers' wreck, and to commemorate it two plays were put on: *This Island's Mine*, based on Shakespeare's *The Tempest*, and *My Heart Stays Here*, based on the *Sea Venture* story. Both names became rallying cries, particularly *This Island's Mine*.

During the year a group of young black people, led by Dr E. Stanley D. Ratteray (later to become a member of the Executive Council) decided that it was time the movie theatres were desegregated, and organized a boycott. It started on the evening of 15 June, and was so successful that on 2 July the theatres were desegregated. There had already been plans to desegregate the theatres when the large new Rosebank Theatre opened in about three months' time, but the group who organized the boycott, who remained anonymous both during it and afterwards, argued that if desegregation could take place in three months' time there was no reason why it should not take place immediately.

The boycott paid an unexpected dividend. The major hotels and most of the restaurants desegregated their public rooms. Among the leaders of the group, in addition to Dr Ratteray, were: Mr Clifford

Wade, Mr and Mrs Rudolph Commissiong, Mr and Mrs Lancelot Swan, Mr William Francis, Mr Coleridge Williams, Mr Eldridge Woods, Mr Gerald Harvey and Mr and Mrs Edward Williams. The year 1959 marked an important turning point. After that white-owned firms which had only employed white people in offices and behind counters started employing black people in these positions too, following the slow lead the Civil Service had given a few years earlier. A barrier more than three centuries old had gone down.

In the same year, and before the boycott, Mr W.L. Tucker was made a member of the Executive Council, the first black man to achieve this position. He was already chairman of a committee which was considering if, and how, the franchise should be extended. In May 1960 his committee made an interim report urging that the franchise should be based on the size of a lot of land, not its value, that leaseholders should have the right to vote, and that plural voting (voting in more than one parish if land was owned in more than one) should be ended.

Movement for Universal Adult Suffrage

It was a compromise, but Bermuda was changing faster than that. There was a great deal of disappointment that the committee had not called for a greater widening of the franchise, and a group of people formed the Committee for Universal Adult Suffrage. Leader of the group and moving force behind it was Mr Roosevelt Brown, who later became an activist for black people in other parts of the world, and leading members were Mr Mansfield Brock, Mr Edward DeJean, Dr Ratteray, Mr Walter Robinson, Mr Coleridge Williams and Mr Leon Williams. The public battle was led by Mr Brown. For two months he acted as chairman of a series of meetings at which the views both of people who wanted 'one person, one vote' and those who wished to retain the land franchise were given.

Working behind the scenes, and then in front of them when he was appointed a member of the Legislative Council and later the Executive Council, was Dr Eustace Cann, who played a vital part in inspiring and advising the leaders of the movement. Slowly the CUAS made progress, until large numbers of people were attending its meetings. While the meetings were continuing a fresh idea was proposed, the 'plus vote'. Under this scheme everyone would have a vote, but landowners, college graduates, people who had served in the armed forces, and those who had attained certain other qualifications, would be given an additional vote for each qualification.

When the meetings ended there was a period of calm on the political front as the community digested the importance of the CUAS meetings. Mr Tucker himself was suffering from a serious illness which in a few years was to take his life. Progress continued, however. In May 1961 a bill was passed preventing restaurants from discriminating between individuals on the basis of race, creed or colour. This important bill was the work of a legislative committee chaired by Mr E.T. Richards. On 14 June the franchise committee reported again. This time the majority of the committee recommended universal suffrage at the age of 21, but a minority called for the voting age to be raised to 25 and that electoral districts be set up with the idea of ensuring that the white minority of Bermudians should be 'protected'.

It was not until 1963 that the new franchise bill became law. Under it every adult over 25 had a vote; the island was divided into 18 electoral districts (two for each parish); and landowners gained an additional 'plus' vote.

Development of Political Parties

The election that year saw the birth of the first modern political party, the Progressive Labour Party. Opposing it during the election was a loose group know as the 'Voters' Association'. The PLP gained six seats, putting five black and one white member into the House. Six other black people also won seats. Soon after the new Assembly started work the United Bermuda Party was formed and gained the support of 24 MCPs, thus controlling the House.

The UBP, like the PLP before it, was formed as a party embracing both races. They chose Sir Henry Tucker as their leader. Long active in Bermuda politics, Sir Henry, a banker, had played a vital part in the behind-the-scenes negotiations which led to universal adult suffrage. A leading member of the white group who wielded the greatest amount of power, he appreciated the need for Bermuda to alter, and was not, like many other white people, afraid that political change would mean trouble and economic setbacks for the island. Indeed, it may well be that he felt that failure to reach agreement would be even more damaging to Bermuda's advancing economy – a pragmatic decision.

Dr Gordon was the man who gave the big push to change: Sir Henry was the man who accepted it, and between them life in Bermuda was moulded into a new way of doing things. The UBP quickly decided that the time had come for a change of Bermuda's ancient unwritten constitution. They also decided to abolish the plus vote and reduce the voting age to 21. These changes were made and a joint select committee of the House and Legislative Council was set up to consider a new constitution.

In November 1966 three members of the Council and 15 of the House met in London with Mr Fred Lee, Secretary of State for the Colonies and Mr John Stonehouse, parliamentary Under-Secretary of State, for a constitutional conference. Also present was the Governor, Lord Martonmere. The 15 members of the House were eight members of the UBP, three members of the PLP, and four independents.

The New Constitution

In the end a majority of Bermudians at the talks agreed on a new constitution which brought a cabinet system of government to Bermuda. The principal points of the constitution were that responsibility for all executive aspects of government except foreign affairs, defence and internal security (including the police force) fell on the Executive Council which in turn was responsible to the House of Assembly, which could force members of the Executive Council to resign. The Council was appointed by the Governor who had to follow the suggestions made to him by the government Leader, the leader of the majority group in the House of Assembly. The Legislative Council was also nominated by the Governor, and consisted of 11 members, four appointed at the suggestion of the government leader, two appointed at the suggestion of the Opposition leader, and five by the Governor at his own discretion. It was also agreed at this time that there should be a revision of electoral boundaries, and that four more seats should be given to Pembroke, the most populous parish, raising the number of members of the House to 40.

The change was made in time for the 1968 election, which saw 30 members of the UBP returned to office, ten members of the PLP and no independents. A new political party emerged before the election, the Bermuda Democratic Party, but they failed to win any seats.

Immediately after the election the new constitution came into effect and has continued with no significant changes. Nomenclature has been changed too: the Executive Council is now the Cabinet, the political heads of government departments are Ministers and the Legislative Council is the Senate. In the Senate the number of independent members has been reduced to three and the opposition and government have gained one each – three members and five members respectively. Constituency boundaries are revised from time to time, but remain within parish borders, and moves to replace two person constituencies with single seat ones have failed. Britain has relinquished some of its powers, so that control of the police is shared between the Governor and Minister for Home Affairs, and Bermudians usually are allowed to take part in negotiations with other nations which affect the island.

At the end of 1971 Sir Henry resigned as government leader and was succeeded by Sir Edward Richards, a move widely hailed as showing that the UBP was genuinely bi-racial. Since then the party has continued to win every election under three different leaders: Mr Jack (now Sir John) Sharpe, Mr David (now Sir David) Gibbons and Mr John (now Sir John) Swan.

In 1985 the UBP won a great victory with a total of 31 seats compared to seven for the PLP and two for the newly formed National Liberal Party. In part this was due to Sir John Swan's personal popularity, but also to a serious split in the PLP which saw the main party veering to the political left, losing a number of members who created the new NLP, which won two seats. In a number of constituencies divided votes for opposition candidates left the way open for UBP victories. Mr Gilbert Darrell was elected party leader of the NLP and retained office after the election. But Mrs Lois Browne-Evans, who as head of the Progressive Labour Party had fought so long for so many causes in and out of Parliament, decided to retire after the results came in and Mr Frederick Wade was elected in her place.

In the election of 1993 the Progressive Labour Party made a strong advance, winning 18 seats to the UBP's 22. The following

*Sir Henry Tucker, KBE, JP, MCP,
former government Leader*

*The Hon. Sir Edward Richards,
CBE, MCP, former Premier*

*The Hon. Sir John Sharpe, CBE,
JP, MP, former Premier*

*The Hon J. David Gibbons, JP,
MP, former Premier*

Mr Frederick Wade, MP

Mr Gilbert Darrell, MP

Mrs Lois Browne-Evans, LLB, JP, MP, Leader of the Opposition 1968–72 and 1976–85

The Hon. Sir John W.D. Swan, JP, MP

year, to the intense surprise of most people, Sir John Swan made a first move towards independence by announcing the government's decision to have a Commission of Enquiry look into the question. The Commission report contained many statements in favour of independence, but most of the figures obtained showed that taxes would have to be increased to support it, and the public debate on the issue centred on whether independence would help the economy or hinder it.

Some UBP members suggested that independence was bound to come and it was better to move to independence under a UBP government, but the party was split on the issue. Independence was part of the PLP platform, but they believed it should take place, as in other British colonies, as a result of a parliamentary election, so Mr Wade called for a boycott of the poll. When the referendum was held in 1995, out of the 37 841 persons eligible 22 236 voted (58%), and 5714 (15% of the electorate and 25.7% of those voting) voted for independence, while 16 369 (43.3% of the electorate and 73.6% of those voting) voted against it. There were 153 void ballots.

With the defeat Sir John Swan resigned and Dr David Saul, the able Finance Minister, was picked to take his place. His administration was handicapped by the Macdonald's hamburger battle. The outgoing Premier and one of his cabinet members had set up a company which had obtained permission to acquire a Macdonald's franchise, a quiet change in policy which took Bermuda by surprise and split the UBP again. The matter was accompanied by cries of 'political sleaze', and amid much talk a bill was passed to stop the Macdonald's franchise and any similar ones. After two years Dr Saul resigned and was replaced by a member of his cabinet, Ms Pamela Gordon, a daughter of Dr E.F. Gordon – a fascinating turn of the wheel of fortune.

Ms Gordon showed great promise in pulling the ailing party together as the first months of 1999 – the deadline for a general election – came closer. But the PLP was also preparing itself, despite the long illness and tragic death of Mr Wade in 1995. Mr Wade, who was mourned by political friends and foes alike, had laid a vital foundation on which his successor, Miss Jennifer Smith, a hardworking MP and Shadow Minister of Education, continued to build, leading to the success of 1998.

Will the PLP victory lead to a different Bermuda in the future? The political platforms of the two parties were similar in many

Dr David Saul

respects, with both groups vying for the political centre. Many felt in the aftermath of the PLP's victory that Bermuda would continue on course, keeping the economy vibrant for the prosperity of all her people.

A Glimpse of Dr Gordon

Miss Eva Hodgson, in *Second-class Citizens; First-class Men*, a book which covers much of this period, quotes a poem which meant much to Dr Gordon early in his career. It was entitled 'If I should die', and reveals the sadness of a man who, at that point, felt that he had been deserted by many who should have been his friends.

The Hon. Pamela Gordon, MP

If I should die
How kind you all would grow,
I would not have one foe.
There are no words too beautiful to say
Of one who goes evermore away

The Hon. Miss Jennifer Smith, MP

Across that ebbing tide which has
No flow.
With that new lustre
My good deeds would glow.
If faults were mine, no one would call them so ...
Ah friends! Before my listening ear lies low,
While I can hear and understand, bestow
That gentle treatment and fond love, pray
The lustre of whose late though radiant way
Would gild my grave with mocking light, I know,
If I should die.

SOURCES
Hodgson, *Second-Class Citizens, First-Class Men.*
Hunter, *Beyond the Crossroads.*
Rushe, *Your Bermuda.*
Stewart, *Bermuda, An Economy which Works.*

21

Trade Unions

Trade unions came late to Bermuda, although attempts to put pressure on employers had occurred many times in the past. For instance, in 1863, a group of black people employed in St George's by the southern Confederate government went on strike for higher wages. The Confederate agent, Major Norman Walker, hired white people to do the work instead, but the black workers continued their strike, which escalated when 3000 bales of cotton were destroyed by fire. Guards were stationed by Major Walker. Finally the workers gave in and returned to work.

Mr Ira Philip tells about labour strife in the early 1900s in his book *Freedom Fighters*. In 1903, 250 Jamaican men, women and children were brought to Bermuda to work for the English construction company C.H. Walker & Co. who had the contract to carry out a major extension of the Dockyard. The conditions under which they were brought to Bermuda and lodged were disgraceful, and led to riots. The workers' side was taken by the Rev. Charles V. Monk, an AME minister, who edited a newspaper called the *People's Journal*. One of his editorials led to the Attorney General's bringing a charge of criminal libel.

There was a lengthy trial, at which the Rev. Monk had no defence counsel, for his lawyer, Mr Matthew Henry Spencer-Joseph of Jamaica, died mysteriously the day before the arraignment. The pastor protested at a number of irregular aspects of the trial, but was found guilty and sentenced to four months in prison and a fine of £100. Some years later he left Bermuda. In 1907 this was followed by an effort by Mr C.C. Wilson to form a labour union, which failed, and Bermuda did not have her first trade union until 1919 when the Bermuda Union of Teachers was constituted. The union worked hard to improve conditions for teachers and for better schools. During the 1950s a second union, the Teachers Association of Bermuda, was formed. Eventually the two unions amalgamated, and today are once again named the Bermuda Union of Teachers.

Industrial trade unionism got started much later. Curiously enough, Bermuda trade unionism started partly as a result of employment problems which developed from another group of outside contractors, the US base contractors, during the Second World War. When the Americans planned to build their bases the Bermuda government was told that it was common American practice to pay local rates of pay to workers on bases, as certified by local governments. Soon after, it was discovered that rates at the bases were in excess of Bermuda rates, and the pay for unskilled labourers was accordingly dropped to five shillings a day. This, however, was the cut rate at which labourers had been employed by the Bermuda government when the war and the drastic cut in the tourism business had created considerable unemployment. There was no reason to stick to this low rate, which was increasingly inadequate as prices went up owing to wartime shortages.

A large meeting was held at the Oddfellows Hall in Hamilton on 4 December 1940, with Mr Russell L. Pearman, who was later to become an MCP, in the chair. Those attending agreed to form themselves into the Bermuda Workers Association, a name suggested by Mr Walton St George Brown. Others who played an important role in the formation of the BWA were Mr Gerald Brangman, Mr Henry Stovell and Mr Wycliffe Stovell. The BWA succeeded in improving wage rates at the US bases and then interest in it dwindled, until in 1944 it had only 200 members. It was in that year that Dr Gordon was asked to become president, and under his vigorous leadership the membership increased to 5000 in 1945.

In 1946 Dr Gordon started his campaign to petition for constitutional and social change, and in the same year the Legislature passed Bermuda's first Trade Union and Disputes Act. The first union to register was the BUT. Under the act unions could not be political organisations and as a result the Bermuda Industrial Union was formed out of the membership of the BWA. The BWA continued in being as the political arm for some years, but has now gone out of existence.

The BIU was born, but it was not healthy. It failed to attract many members of the BWA, partly because wages by now had caught up with price increases. Most of the members of the new union were dock workers, and in 1948 they went on strike for higher wages. The stevedoring firms managed to obtain the services of other people, including shop assistants who were released from their normal work by store owners, but in the end there were negotiations between the BIU and management which settled the dispute. The successful outcome of the strike led to an increase in BIU members to just over 1000, but in the year of Dr Gordon's death, 1955, membership suddenly dropped to 26. The events of 1959, however, changed the situation, and membership grew once more. In the same year there was a second dock strike, which reached deadlock while ships continued to be unloaded by non-union labour. The strikers decided to try strong-arm tactics, armed themselves with sticks, and demonstrated outside Police Headquarters (then in Hamilton), later marching on No. 1 Shed. The Riot Act was read twice, and at No. 1 Shed the strikers encountered the police riot squad, the first time such a group had been called out in Bermuda. The confrontation fortunately passed off peacefully, and finally the strikers dispersed. Soon afterwards a number of dock workers formed the Bermuda Dock Workers Union, splitting off from the BIU.

By 1960 there were approximately 900 members in all unions in Bermuda, but this included, because of the way the law was written, the Bermuda Employers Council, a management group.

Turning Point

During the early 1960s the BIU began to mature, sending officers abroad for training and recruiting members. Then, in 1965, came an important turning point in the history of trade unionism in Bermuda when the BIU called on the Bermuda Electric Light Company to recognize them as bargaining agents. The Electric Light Company said it would grant recognition if 60 per cent of its hourly paid workers voted for the union; the union called for more than 50 per cent, and a ballot only of workers in certain sectors of the company's operation. The BIU members came out on strike, and after ten days the union called on three other divisions representing workers in other fields to come out in sympathy. This led to a picket line of some 300 people, and on the fateful 2 February 1965 the growing tensions burst into violence. The police arrested the BIU president and two pickets, and soon afterwards a riot occurred in which one policeman was seriously hurt. The riot squad was called out, and the pickets dispersed to the Devonshire Recreation Club, where they were joined by many others who also downed tools.

What had been a union dispute quickly created racial tensions, and the Reserve Constabulary, the Bermuda Rifles (formerly the Bermuda Volunteer Rifle Corps) and the Bermuda Militia Artillery were mobilized to keep the peace.

During this time non-BIU workers at the Electric Light Company, who were in fact the majority, for the BIU had only 80 members plus a number of sympathizers on the staff of 231, kept electricity flowing to the community. This was a tense time for them, and they formed a rival union, the Electrical Supply Trade Union. The strike ended when the Electric Light Company management agreed to negotiate with whichever union commanded a majority of the workers, and in the subsequent ballot the ESTU won.

It was the worst strike and the worst violence that Bermuda had ever known. The BIU lost the battle, but it won the war. Since then union recognition has normally been based on a simple majority whenever a secret ballot has been taken. The number of members of the BIU increased, and in 1969 some 3494 members were recorded.

At the same time relations between union and management considerably improved. Unions became part of the normal fabric of life, no longer being regarded by managements with suspicion as subversive elements, and unions learned much more about negotiating techniques. By 1969 the BIU reported collective agreements with 63 employers. Total membership in all unions (excluding the Bermuda Employers Council and the Hotel Employers of Bermuda) was nearing the 5000 mark. In 1979 the number of members of all unions had increased to 7071. Generally union-management relations in this period were harmonious, but this was interrupted in April 1981, when the BIU hospital division covering hourly paid workers, struck for better pay. Protracted negotiations had brought no result when the workers decided to strike, but even this trial of strength failed to resolve the deadlock.

It was in April, as the spring tourist season was in full swing, that the hotel workers, who would soon be starting negotiations for a new contract themselves, decided to support the hospital personnel. Other union divisions joined in, and the community was almost brought to a standstill. The hotels decided to close, and then faced the problem of getting the guests to the airport. As the buses were not running and taxi drivers were not willing to face airport picket lines, private car owners volunteered and faced the problem of driving through a mass of people shouting imprecations at them and their passengers. The picket lines themselves were the correct, legal, ten persons only, but the crowds waiting around the entrance to the airport were intimidating.

The situation was sufficiently serious for both the Reserve Constabulary and the Bermuda Regiment to be called up. Finally the strike was settled on 7 May, and efforts were made to rebuild the tourist trade, but the rest of the year was a period of depression. This had a marked effect on the hotel negotiations which were completed far more quickly than on previous occasions.

In 1996 the total number of persons registered as members of trade unions was 8054. A union which has grown in the last 30 years under the leadership of Mr Eugene Blakeney – General Secretary from 1979 until he retired – is the Bermuda Public Services Association, which had 2476 members in 1966 as compared to the BIU's 4117 in the same year. The BPSA was originally formed from members of the Civil Service. Now the BPSA has branched out and represents several groups of white collar workers as well. Late in 1997 Mr Blakeney announced his impending retirement.

Personalities

The most notable figure in the trade union story to date has been, after the towering figure of Dr Gordon, Mr Ottiwell A. Simmons. Mr Simmons was elected President in 1981 and held this post for over a decade when he was succeeded by Mr Derrick Burgess in 1996. His leadership saw the Union start the BIU Credit Union, the Bermuda Co-op Supermarket and the Liberty Theatre. Although the union continued to show its strength during this period, industrial relations were generally good, often with indications that there had been careful negotiations behind the scenes. As an MP Ottiwell

Mr Derrick Burgess, President of the Bermuda Industrial Union

Simmons became a leading personality in the Progressive Labour Party.

Others who played an important role in the rise of trade unions include Mr Ira Philip, who succeeded Dr Gordon as Secretary-General, Mr Martin T. Wilson, who was President during some of the most difficult times; Mr Robert T. Johnston, long-term, President; Dr Barbara Ball who joined the BIU in the early 1960s and became Secretary-General, a post she held for many years, relinquishing it to become Research officer for the BIU; Mr Eugene Blakeney, who was with the BIU before going to the BPSA, and Mr Reid Simmons.

*Mr Ottiwell A. Simmons, former President of the
Bermuda Industrial Union*

Bermuda has never had a closed shop, but to ensure that union employees of firms which have union agreements are not singled out in having pay deductions, the BIU won the concession of 'agency shops'. Under agency shop agreements all employees have union dues deducted from their pay, but can elect to have the pay donated to charity instead of going to the union. Pay deductions sent directly to the BIU helped to improve union finances, so that more permanent staff could be hired to handle bargaining sessions and disputes.

SOURCES
Barclay (ed.), *Bermuda Business Who's Who.*
Hunter, *Beyond the Crossroads.*
Philip, *Freedom Fighters – from Monk to Mazumbo.*
Rushe, *Your Bermuda.*
Stewart, *Bermuda, An Economy which Works.*

22

The Story of Education

The period of change from the end of the Second World War to the present was as marked in education as it was in many other areas of life in Bermuda, and there have been two distinct eras of reform. However, the history of education goes back much further than that. Many members of the Bermuda Company and many early settlers had absorbed the views of the Puritans in England. The Puritans believed in education, and among their early actions in New England, for instance, was the establishment of Harvard College, to which Bermudians contributed.

In Bermuda the Company decided to set aside land for school purposes, and one of the shareholders, Sir Nathaniel Rich, gave nearly half his shares of land to be occupied by a school and to help maintain it. Sir Nathaniel thought a school in Bermuda would be useful for training Indians from the mainland as well as Bermudians, a scheme which, with variations, was to crop up several more times.

In 1663 three schoolhouses were built. Each was 14 feet by 16 feet and provided with a chimney. One of these still exists and forms part of Warwick Academy. Richard Norwood, the surveyor, was the most notable Bermuda schoolteacher of the era. He had taught in England, and was the author of several books on mathematics.

After the Company era interest in education seems to have waned. Bermuda's leaders were not educated men, and teaching became a second job for the clergy, helped by other people from time to time. Nathaniel Tucker gives an idea of what education was like in part of his poem *The Bermudian*, written shortly before the American Revolution. He paints a picture of a master patting a switch in his hands while his pupils worked out their sums or read their Latin out loud – a busy cacophony of sound.

> Near yonder hill, above the stagnant pool,
> My stern preceptor taught his little school;
> Dextrous t'apply the scientifik rod,
> The little truants shuddered at his nod;
> Whene'er he came, they all submissive bow'd,
> All scann'd their tasks, industriously loud,
> And, fearful to excite the master's rage,
> With trembling hands produc'd the blotted page.

There was one far-reaching plan which might have helped Bermuda education enormously, a scheme conceived in England by Bishop George Berkeley. On 1 June 1725, the Bishop obtained a charter from King George I to build a college known as St Paul's in Bermuda. St Paul's would have educated Americans and Indians as well as Bermudians up to Master of Arts standard. Unfortunately the money was not forthcoming, and although the Bishop crossed the Atlantic and lived for a period in Rhode Island he never reached Bermuda. But a period of change was on the way, and as the 18th century reached its end the Rev. John Stephenson arrived on the island.

Missionary Education

Stephenson was a Methodist, and the Methodists, like their Puritan predecessors of the previous century, were interested in education. Although Stephenson was hounded out of the island, as related earlier, he was succeeded by the Rev. Joshua Marsden who began to educate poor people and slaves. Other Methodist ministers followed, and by 1832 the Methodists had nine Sunday Schools functioning, staffed by 50 white and 16 black teachers with 283 slave children and 96 white children attending. These Sunday Schools taught reading and writing as well as the scriptures.

The Church of England followed the Methodists into education, and at the time of Harriet Suzette Lloyd's visit just before the end of slavery (1829–31) Archdeadon (later Bishop) Spencer had set up a number of schools and 1000 black people were receiving instruction in them. Archdeacon Spencer, who did much to mould the Bermuda community in the mid-19th century, was assisted from England by the Society for the Religious Instruction of Negroes.

Government and Education

In 1837 the Chief Justice, John Christie Esten, proposed a radical plan for the education of all children in Bermuda, arguing that the training of children of former slaves was a moral obligation on white people. He wrote:

> ... through seven generations have they not been our obedient and attached slaves? For us and our ancestors they have risen early and late taken rest; they toiled through the live-long summer's day and in the sweat of their faces they have eaten the bread which we have provided for them. Their food was cheap, their clothes inexpensive, we have been enriched by the fruits of their labour; we have brought up our sons and our daughters and lived, many of us, in the enjoyment of luxuries ... at our bidding they have undergone fatigue and labour; at our command they have periled themselves on the ocean and hundreds and thousands have perished in the deep. And, in return for all these sacrifices, what do their children of the present generation demand of us?

The government would not swallow Esten's far-reaching plan, but in 1839 the first general grant for education of white and black was made, and from then on, apart from a short period between 1860 and 1866, government continued to help education. That short period included the American Civil War, when Major Norman Walker and his wife Georgianna were here. Mrs Walker, in her private journal, told about their experiences soon after her arrival in 1863:

> The first news I get of any unusual event, such as a wedding or a funeral, is from the children, who rush home in great excitement, saying school has broken up and teacher has gone to the 'Sight'.

New Schools

St Paul's

In 1855 a new school was opened which was meant to carry on part of Bishop Berkeley's plan. The man behind it was the Rev. William C. Dowding, and his idea was to build a non-segregated school which would offer education not only to Bermudians but also to people from the West Indies. Rev. Dowding obtained help from a number of prominent British sponsors, including the Archbishop of Canterbury, and with funds in hand came to Bermuda, hired a building, and started the school, which he called St Paul's after Bishop Berkeley's proposed institution. The school started with mainly black pupils and some white, but it came under severe attack from a number of prominent white people. Dowding was forced to return to England to try and obtain more financial support, but in 1856 the school was closed down.

Devonshire College

Earlier in the century an attempt was made to open a superior school for white boys. What could be saved of the old Bermuda Company schools lands were placed under a body of trustees. The trustees managed to sell much of the land, and devoted the proceeds to building a school in Devonshire. This was the Devonshire College. It was opened in 1829 but after a few years proved to be a failure. Some of the buildings still stand, however, and are now part of St Brendan's Hospital.

Later on it was decided to turn the money over to two groups of trustees, known as 'Bodies'; Body No. 1 to run a school for white boys, and Body No. 2 to run a school for black boys. The school for white boys became Saltus Grammar School, which opened in 1887 in Pembroke Sunday School and two years later moved to its own premises. The second scheme ran into opposition, for many black people argued that the Devonshire College money should be kept together for an integrated school. The argument dragged on for many years, but before it was resolved the Berkeley Educational Society had been founded with the idea of opening an integrated school. The society was formed by black people, but soon after its beginning was joined by several white people, including the Rector of Pembroke, the Rev. Mark James.

After a long struggle the Society succeeded in opening the school at Samaritans's Hall, Hamilton, on 1 September 1897, with Mr George A. DeCosta as the first headmaster, and 27 pupils, one of whom was white. For many years interest derived from the Devonshire College Body No. 2 money was used to provide secondary school scholarships, but in 1933 the capital was turned over to Berkeley for additions and alterations.

More schools

Many of the schools extant today were started around the end of the 19th century, among them Sandys Grammar School, the Bermuda High School for Girls, Mount St Agnes, Whitney Institute and St George's Grammar School. The schools started as white schools and were built through the efforts of interested groups. The Whitney, for instance, was built by neighbourhood fund raising. Construction was well under way when a hurricane destroyed much of the work. But two neighbours, Mr and Mrs Whitney, gave money to make up for the loss, and the school was completed.

At the same time the government was taking an increasing interest in education. An Act passed in 1879 provided for the continuation of the Board of Education, and an Inspector of Schools, but also added local parish school boards. In 1881 there were 21 schools under the control of the Board of Education, which were inspected by a man who left his mark on Bermuda education. George Simpson was a tyrant, and ruled schools with such a rod of iron that he even specified what pieces of poetry should be learned. He continued in his post well into the 20th century.

'He was short in stature,' wrote Mr Edward York in an article published by the *Bermuda Historical Quarterly,*

> and was possessed of considerable embonpoint. His bald head contrasted strongly with extremely shaggy eyebrows, a 'Robertson Hare' moustache, and a pair of bright corn-blue eyes which gazed menacingly at a boy from behind a pair of gold-rimmed spectacles. Letting his keen glance wander about the class, he reminded one of the giant Polyphemus speculating on whom next to devour.

The eyes fell on Mr York, who had to read out loud, but fortunately carried it off successfully. During the 1920s, 1930s, and 1940s the school system grew only gradually, one of the most noteworthy events being the setting up from 1931 of grants for teachers to train abroad. In the late 1940s this began to produce considerable fruit, giving great impetus to the development of a black professional class. Many teachers went on to other jobs and professions, but their start was gained through the teacher training programme.

The other big advance came in 1949 when, after a long struggle, free primary education was introduced. Education was, however, compulsory only from the ages of seven to 13, as it had been for many years. It was not until the 1960s that the period was lengthened, at first from five to 15 years, and then to the present five to 16 years. By then most children were being educated for longer periods anyway.

Despite the teacher-training programme, men and women were constantly brought in from abroad to provide enough teachers. They came mainly from Britain and the West Indies.

Howard Academy

From the mid-1930s on the only two schools giving secondary education to black children were Berkeley Institute and newly opened Sandys Secondary School which had to struggle against many difficulties. Then, in the 1940s, came the battle of Howard Academy.

The Academy was started in mid-decade when Mr Edward Skinner, a former headmaster of Cavendish School, started tutoring youngsters in his home. It was quickly discovered that there was a heavy demand for secondary education for students who were unable to obtain places in Berkeley and Sandys. Parents banded together to enlarge the school, giving their labour to build additional facilities. The government was asked for help, but showed little willingness to oblige. Eventually an area of land at Prospect and a stone building was provided in 1953, and parents added a surplus wooden building obtained from the Royal Navy Dockyard.

In 1956 the decision to build the Technical Institute – designed to replace the Dockyard Apprenticeship scheme and the first post-war school to be declared bi-racial by the government – on the Howard site meant another move. Wooden buildings and a nearby site were provided, and once more parents turned to and erected a new school.

By this time government had come to acknowledge the intense longing in the island for secondary education, and, with the spark provided by Howard, St George's Secondary School was opened, to be followed by others. These new secondary schools were not expected to produce college-entrance graduates, but in fact many of them did so.

The arrival of other secondary schools meant the end of the Howard scheme. In 1965 the government grant was withdrawn and Howard closed its doors. But many of the pupils, particularly those educated under the dynamic Mr Edward DeJean, have played important roles in the community, typified by Sir John Swan, who rose not only to be Premier but also a highly successful businessman.

Academic Schools

During the same year government support for racially segregated schools was withdrawn, although by this time a number of white schools had dropped racial barriers anyway. No black schools had formal racial barriers. At the same time the education authorities decided that Berkeley, Saltus and Warwick Academy were to take special responsibility for college-entrance training, while the remaining secondary schools would concentrate on vocational training. Secondary school placement examinations were used by the schools as a guide to the pupils they accepted.

The previous year the Bermuda High School for Girls had decided to leave the government system and become a private school. In doing this they joined a number of small schools and Mount St Agnes, which had never received outright government money. The High School left the system because they did not believe in the idea of separating likely college-entrance children from other children – and over a period of time others began to think they were right.

Some years later, in 1970, Saltus also decided to become a private school after a lengthy battle over the question of the Saltus primary school being run directly by the government instead of falling under the wing of the Saltus Trustees. The question developed out of moves to promote more integration of school populations by amalgamating mainly white primary schools with mainly back ones. Saltus primary was to have amalgamated with Northlands, at that point a primary school (an idea suggested by the Saltus Trustees) but government opinion was that the new school should come directly under the Department of Education. The Saltus Trustees disagreed, and finally took the entire school out of the system.

In 1967 a brand new school in premises built for the purpose, Warwick Secondary, was opened, and during the late 1960s the government also decided to set up a separate centre for students working for General Certificate of Education 'A' levels, and the Sixth Form Centre was born. It met first in Pembroke Sunday School, then moved to a new school building in Prospect. The establishment of the Sixth Form Centre was followed by a decision to turn the Technical Institute into another post-secondary school, following the lead already given by the Bermuda Hotel and Catering College. The Hotel College traced its origins back to the Domestic Science Centre which was started in 1936 to provide training in looking after the home and also in hotel and domestic service. In the post-war years these functions were split. Home training was worked into the curriculum of all the schools and the Hotel School was set up to train Bermudians in hotel work.

In 1972 the three post-secondary schools were joined together and renamed the Bermuda College, giving Bermuda the equivalent of an American junior college. Although the name 'college' seemed grandiose at the time, the Bermuda College has played an increasingly important role in Bermuda. It has set high standards for its principal courses, and organized evening courses designed for the direct needs of people trying to improve their knowledge and skills in the arts, business and trades. Other night courses, many of a more recreational nature, are given in several schools under the aegis of the Department of Youth, Sport and Recreation.

Full college-level education came to Bermuda in a limited way through the University of Maryland, which started night classes at the US Naval Air Station. At the same time Queen's University in Canada became noted for its correspondence courses, and also ran summer courses in Bermuda. In 1981 three US Colleges were operating courses at the base.

From time to time there are revivals of the old schemes to open a school to attract American and other outside students, but all such projects which have actually started have failed after a few years of operation. Bishop Berkeley's dream remains to be fulfilled.

However, the fine new college on its campus in Paget would certainly have met the Bishop's dreams for a splendid colonial school.

The Educational Planning Team

The concern expressed by the Bermuda High School for Girls at the outset of the separate academic school era proved to be a potent question as students attending the general secondary schools increasingly felt themselves to be second-rate persons, a problem which had developed in Britain as well. In addition, it was found that the number of girls qualifying for the Academic Schools greatly exceeded the number of boys, and many felt it was because boys, broadly speaking, developed an ability to benefit from education at a later age than girls.

One solution tried in Britain was the Comprehensive School. These were large schools designed to cater to a broad range of abilities where a pupil who was good in English but poor in maths could be placed in courses suitable for his or her talents. On the other hand there was anecdotal evidence from Britain that the comprehensives had many problems.

What was to be done? The Minister of Education, the Hon. Gerald Simons, MP, decided to obtain a large measure of public input into the problem. He and the Permanent Secretary, Dr Marion Robinson, had heard of the work of an American counsultancy company which sought to bring together people with differing viewpoints to obtain a consensus acceptable to the community. A group of interested persons was formed and a long series of meetings held. In March 1989, the Educational Planning Team gave its report, which recommended the establishment of Middle Schools and Senior Secondary Schools. Under the scheme the top forms of the Primary Schools would be amalgamated with the lower forms of the Secondary Schools to form Middle Schools, a concept developed to improve on the American Junior High Schools. The EPT made many other recommendations as well.

Much information was gained from Canada, and the Minister and the majority of the EPT were persuaded by a Canadian expert that one Senior Secondary School would give the island a facility which would contain the best teachers, laboratories and other facilities which could be provided – something which would not be

Warwick Academy

possible if there were several senior secondaries. The obvious central place to put it would be at Prospect.

Many Bermudians were concerned about the idea of a large school without any competition, and the scheme was heavily criticized. Berkeley's loyal graduates were particularly annoyed at the idea of their school becoming a Middle School. Warwick Academy, already unhappy with the idea of losing its status as an academic secondary, decided to leave the government educational system entirely, and in September 1992 opened as a private fee-paying school.

Finally it was agreed that there should be two senior secondaries – Berkeley and a new campus planned for Prospect, called Cedarbridge Academy, but the uproar, coupled with severe disciplinary problems in several schools, led to more people struggling to find the money to pay for private education. By 1996 only 66 per cent of Bermuda children were in public schools.

At the time of writing in 1997 the new education plan, after many problems, is about to get under way. Mr Gerald Simons, who came under much criticism about the new system and the problems of the old, said it was like building a house while you were living in it. Eventually he resigned and then, having lost his seat in the 1993 election, left politics, but the government has carried on with the scheme in the optimistic hope that it will improve education in Bermuda. Meanwhile a quieter revolution had taken place. Improvements in teachers' salaries and the continuation of training schemes mean that as the century nears its end nearly all Bermuda's teachers are Bermudian.

SOURCES
Bermuda Historical Quarterly, Vol. 20, No. 1 (Spring 1963).
Hunter, *Beyond the Crossroads*.
Lloyd, *Sketches of Bermuda*.
Robinson, unpublished thesis on the history of education.
Rushe, *Your Bermuda*.
Stewart, *Bermuda, an Economy which Works*.
Tucker, *The Bermudian*.
Walker (ed. Dwight Franklin Henderson), *The Private Journal of Georgiana Gholson Walker, 1852–1865*.

23

Arts and Crafts

The Bermuda people have developed only two forms of art: architecture and Gombey dancing. That there are only two is not surprising – what *is* surprising is that any developed at all, for Bermuda is not a large place, and throughout its history has been swayed by influences reaching it from North America, Great Britain, the West Indies and Africa.

Architecture

Some of the original architectural forms sprang from the west of England, but local conditions and local materials brought important modifications. The first important stone building, the State House, erected by Governor Nathaniel Butler, was not based on English traditions but was built in a Mediterranean style. The Governor's idea was to make the walls out of stone and thick, to withstand hurricane winds and keep out the heat, and to have a flat roof and make that out of stone, too. As it was a public building he apparently felt that it should have some decoration, and today the restored State House once again has a decorative entrance and a flat roof.

The stone idea was an excellent one. Bermuda stone was easy to quarry and cut into good-sized building blocks, and after a time the dimensions became standard – 24 inches long by six, eight or 12 inches wide, depending on where the stone was to be used, whether for the foundations, first floor or second floor. The flat roof, however, was a poor idea. Heavy rains easily penetrated the

A characteristic Bermuda chimney graces the
St George's Historical Society building on Featherbed
Alley, St George's

porous stone even when it was washed with lime, and a steep roof
was needed to throw off the water. Chimneys were an important
part of the building, for fireplaces were needed for cooking and
winter heating, and at first, following the English fashion, they were
placed inside the building. But during the long summer cooking fires
had to be kept going and the heat must have been a trial. That was
apparently the reason why the characteristic outside Bermuda
chimney developed, with its broad base leaving room for the
fireplace opening inside the house, and then a long narrowing reach
upwards on the wall of the building until it reaches full height
several feet above the roof line.

In the largest houses the Bermudians followed the Virginia
fashion of having the kitchen in a separate building because of the
heat and smells, and the risk of fire. Sometimes the kitchens might
even be rented to another house – and the kitchen of the Tucker
House in St George's became Joseph Hayne Rainey's barbershop

State House in St George's, the oldest public building
in Bermuda, whose reconstruction was completed in
1970; it now resembles the illustration in Smith's
History of Virginia

during the American Civil War. No doubt the cooking fireplace was used to warm water for shaving.

Inside the house the steep roof with its heavy rafters and bracing led architects to use low walls, and then part of the roof space for a ceiling – the crossties made it impossible to build attics. These tray ceilings, following the line of the rafters, perched on top of walls no higher than the door and window frames.

During the slavery period builders worked out accommodation for slaves, and many old buildings contain semi-basements sunk partly below floor level. These could be used for storage or for housing slaves, while the family lived on the upper level, reached by a sweeping set of stairs. These were traditionally flared at the bottom and are known as 'welcoming arms' stairs. Slaves did not always live in the basement; sometimes they had separate cottages.

At first Bermuda homes were frame built. Cedar posts dug in the ground were linked by beams, and the spaces between were filled with wattle-and-daub – small sticks and plaster. It seems likely that the posts of these houses were rotting in the ground by the early 18th century when Bermuda was hit by severe hurricanes. Certainly many of the early churches were knocked down and rebuilt in stone at that time, and it seems likely that dwellings followed the same course.

The houses were not always carefully planned. Sometimes a couple setting up housekeeping would start with enough rooms for themselves, then add on additional rooms as their families grew bigger. Houses often had a number of outbuildings, including the characteristic buttery. This building was designed with a high roof reaching a point, and usually surmounted by a stone ball. The high roof would help to keep the building cool, and thus it would be more suitable for storing food. In addition, such roofs on small buildings did not require rafters, and the buildings were also used for other purposes, including privies – earth toilets in separate buildings.

Water was always a problem, and the idea of catching water on roofs and leading it into tanks must have arrived early in Bermuda's history. It seems likely that Bermudians (like most Western people) rarely washed themselves in times past, so the tanks were probably small. Quite when the old fashioned round-top tank came into use is not known, but it was probably after many of the houses were built, for the round-tops grew to a fair size. A particular advantage was that their arched roofs could be made entirely of stone without rafters and the gable end made a convenient place for a window through which one could dip water with a bucket.

Most of the houses had small windows made with thick frames to ensure strength against hurricanes. An old picture of St George's indicates that at first they had diamond panes, and therefore probably casement (side-hinged) windows. Later the Georgian double-hung sash window came into use, at first without sash cords. Blinds appear to have been made of boards fastened together, for jalousie blinds apparently did not reach Bermuda until early in the 19th century. They soon became popular, providing safety for the glass windows and ventilation at the same time. Summer verandahs shuttered with jalousie blinds were added to a number of houses. Cedar trees must have helped to dictate the size of houses, for the difficulty of finding tall enough trees to provide stout beams over 16 feet in length helped to limit the building's width.

During the 18th century Bermuda houses often developed graceful lines and proportions, but the 19th century saw buildings falling under the influence of Victorian artistic ideas. In Britain and America it was a time when the development of factories for making a wide variety of objects began to help people to obtain fancy decorative material, which in turn led to many fresh architectural fancies. Some products of the age are unattractive, but in the last few decades a change has occurred in public taste. What the post-Victorian world regarded as overdone many people now feel has the attraction of the antique. Many old houses were simply painted with limewash which gradually became a stucco, but with the development of cement plaster became the norm. Until after the Second World War the usual paint for roofs and walls was limewash. The lime was made in Bermuda by cooking limestone rock over a slow-burning fire.

The twentieth century has seen a return to the simpler aesthetic views of the 18th century in a movement which was led by Wilfred Onions, an architect who studied the island's 18th century buildings and developed a style which incorporated many attractive details of that period while turning out interiors with pleasant proportions designed for 20th century living. His largest building was the Hamilton City Hall, which adapted Bermuda house-style to a large building.

Since the Second World War some of the ideas of modern architects elsewhere have been imported, and much of Hamilton has been converted to various forms of international modern architecture. There are pleasing examples, but many of them are devoid of attraction.

Gombeys

Gombeys date back to at least the mid-18th century, as is shown by the banning of their festivities after the trouble of 1761, but by the time of Harriet Suzette Lloyd's visit just before the end of slavery they were once again an exciting part of the Bermuda scene. According to Mrs Albert Jackson, a dancer herself, the Gombey dances are an amalgamation of many different influences, from Africa, Britain, the West Indies and from American Indians.

At one time the Gombeys danced with high headdresses made in many forms – a Noah's Ark, a house, a boat, an aeroplane – but more recently height has been gained by using peacock feathers. Costumes are still as colourful as they were when Harriett Lloyd saw them, and nowadays are often decorated with large numbers of small mirrors. Although marching bands no longer accompany the dancers, the military drums remain. Most Bermudians are entranced by the Gombeys, and turn out in large crowds when the sound of the drum, whistle and pounding feet are heard.

Gombey dancers

Crafts

Although original ways of creating artistic forms were strictly limited in Bermuda, the island through its history produced many able craftsmen. Woodworkers had the good fortune of having cedar with which to make furniture, for the wood takes on a deep lustre when carefully smoothed and polished. Time slowly darkens the cedar, so that some of the oldest pieces are almost black. It is a brittle wood which makes it difficult to use for delicate table and chair legs, but even this difficulty has been overcome by skilled persons. Other woods were brought to Bermuda and used, notably mahogany, but also pitch-pine, which takes on a mellow light-brown hue with age. Bermuda also produced a number of able silver-smiths, and today Bermuda-made silver is rare and valuable.

Was the Bermuda rig, and were Bermuda-designed vessels a matter of an art or a craft? The question can be argued from either side. Certainly during the 19th century Bermuda vessels were noted for their speed which must have been the result of good designing: in those days this was done by a man with a knife who whittled a

Examples of Bermuda silver

'half-model' – one side of a ship from bow to stern stuck on a board. Some half-models have been preserved and can still be seen in museums.

An English officer stationed in Bermuda in the 19th century was delighted with Bermuda sailboats, but their sailing qualities frightened some people. One day he offered to take an American ship captain from Ireland Island to Hamilton. 'It was blowing a fresh breeze, no more,' the officer wrote.

> Before the boat had got out of the camber (enclosed breakwater) a puff of wind caused it to lean over for a moment. Although the worthy skipper had just undergone the ordeal of a very rough passage from America he almost lost his head in fright.
>
> He gave a positive shout of terror as he abandoned his seat on the hatchway. He was answered by a shout of laughter from two young fellow passengers of the army and marines. But Jonathan [a last-century name for all Americans] recovered himself, and exclaimed: 'I'm no coward, but I don't like to take risks.'

Today a form of the Bermuda rig is used on sailing yachts all over the world. In Bermuda an older version gets a workout on dinghy-racing days, when small open boats, heavily overloaded with canvas and manned by large crews, fight for special trophies. One man is the bailer and is constantly at work. If the wind drops the captain is permitted to reduce the number of the crew; naturally each person goes to the rear and dives off the stern, giving the dinghy a good hard push.

Other Arts

Painting

In the mid-18th century Bermuda was visited by Joseph Blackburn, an English painter who stayed here for a period painting portraits of members of wealthy families before going on to the other colonies, such as Massachusetts, where several of his works are preserved in the Boston Museum of Fine Arts. The occasional itinerant portraitist seems to have been the only contact Bermudians had with art in much of the 18th century. In the 19th century, however,

*Bermuda-fitted dinghies carry on a long tradition of
boat-building on the island*

this changed as the garrison increased. A number of army officers
were trained in military sketching, and in any case painting land-
scapes came to be a hobby with many persons. Among the most
notable 19th century painters of Bermuda scenes are Thomas Driver,
E.G. Hallewell and Edward James. There were a number of women
painters as well, including Princess Louise herself and Lady Lefroy,
wife of the Governor-historian. Most of the Bermuda paintings of
the period are cared for by the Bermuda Archives, except those of
Princess Louise, which are in Canada.

After the Second World War Bermuda artists started to band
together in associations to help sell their works. At the time of
writing the Bermuda Society of Arts is the premier organization,
with a major gallery at the City Hall, while the Bermuda Arts Centre
at the Dockyard has a gallery there. Both are active promoters of
paintings, but in recent years they have been joined by two other

organizations. The Bermuda National Gallery opened on 15 March 1992, and has a charming two-storey premises in the City Hall. Many of the works were collected by Bermudians but are not pictures of Bermuda, and there is often a travelling or special exhibition in the rooms. A good many of the paintings of Bermuda belong to the other organization, the Masterworks Foundation, led by Tom Butterfield, which since 1987 has indefatigably collected 500 paintings of Bermuda by artists such as Winslow Homer, Georgia O'Keefe, Charles DeMuth, Albert Gleizes and Ogden Pleissner.

It is a sign of the advance of painting that a number of persons are able to make a living through their artistry.

Performing Arts

The performing arts have been blessed with the foundation of the Bermuda Festival in 1975, which every year brings actors and musicians to Bermuda. Many of the performances are rapidly sold out soon after the tickets become available. Generally the Festival has taken place in the City Hall Theatre, but this charming theatre has not always been large enough to meet the demand. Now the advent of larger school auditoriums with seating for 600 or more should open up the presentations to larger audiences. It has taken many years to find a true replacement for the Colonial Opera House, which was built for the production of plays and musicals and then became a movie house before its last bow as a church.

Books

In recent years there has been a considerable development in books by Bermuda authors. The Bermudian Publishing Co. and the Island Press have published a number of titles, while the Bermuda Maritime Museum and the Bermuda National Trust have contributed books pertaining to their particular areas. A good many authors have published books themselves, while others have been taken under the wing of the Writers' Machine, founded in 1978 by Dale Butler. By 1997 28 titles had been published. Mr Butler remembers particularly the year 1994 when, in honour of the 50th anniversary of female suffrage in Bermuda, he introduced a number of volumes with his 'book a night' event.

SOURCES
Lloyd, *Sketches of Bermuda*.
A Field Officer (Major Whittingham) *Bermuda, a Colony, a Fortress and a Prison.*

Transition:
The Future

Bermuda's motto is *Quo Fata Ferunt*, 'Whither the fates lead us', an appropriate statement for a small community facing a large and changing world as the globe rolls on to the next millenium.

Thinking in terms of the next two hundred years or so, the global economy faces many difficulties and opportunities –

- Difficulties such as an ever-growing population and problems of food and housing for people; depletion of natural resources; and an endangered environment through loss of the ozone layer and global warming.
- Opportunities such as a continuing tide of scientific advance coupled with growing interest in space exploration and improving health for all people; and a world growing smaller through rapid communications and increased contact.

How will Bermuda fit in to these changes? The fates have recently lead to the withdrawal of soldiers, sailors and airmen of Britain, Canada and the United States making land available that will put off the time when a growing population will force us to answer a basic question: Should we increase the land area of the island by further expansion into the ocean? The large areas of shallow water in the great North lagoon could be used for development. Such development, however, would be dangerous to the life of the coral reef which, for our safety, must live and build because it is constantly being worn away. Jamaica has lost 94% of its coral reef through mismanagement, a dreadful warning.

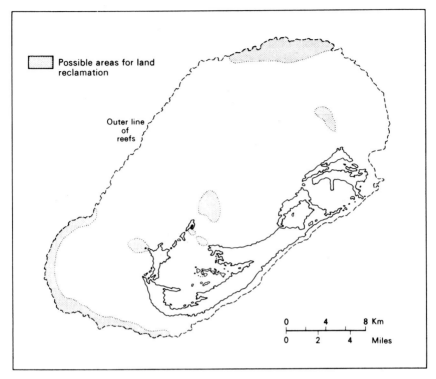

Land for possible reclamation identified in the 1970s

Small communities are prone to keep the same group in power for long periods of time, but in democracies change comes eventually, and when it does there will be a number of superficial changes as new hands learn the powers and problems of governance. Sooner or later, no matter which party is in power, the question of whether Bermuda should remain a colony of Britain will come up again, perhaps because Britain will decide it no longer wishes to have any distant dependencies.

An increasing world population means that we are likely to face greater pressures to take more immigrants, whether as inexpensive domestic and garden workers or as experts in the trades which support our economy. No doubt more Bermudians will want to emigrate as well, which means that education will continue to be of the utmost importance to Bermudians.

Will we experience a resurgence in tourism, or will the offshore company business support an ever-growing percentage of our economy? And if this occurs will there be work for everyone? Other more esoteric possibilities may be of importance in the future, including deep sea mining within the economic zone allocated to Bermuda.

No one wants it, but the possibility of global war cannot be excluded. Any fighting affecting the North Atlantic affects us, and could change many aspects of our lives. We have been called 'the nimble Bermudians' and we may have to be nimble in our thinking and actions as the world changes. *Quo Fata Ferunt!*

The Royal Navy Dockyard today, with the Commissioner's House and the Maritime Museum at the far end

Bibliography

Books

Barclay, Charles (ed.), *Bermuda Business Who's Who*. Bermuda: Bermuda Marketing Ltd, 1997.

Block, Dolores G., *Kindley Air Force Base, Bermuda – The First 25 Years*. Unpublished MS, 1969.

Britton, Nathaniel Lord, *Flora of Bermuda*. New York, Charles Scribner's Sons, 1918.

Bowler, R. Arthur, *Logistics and the Failure of the British Army in America 1775–1783*. Princeton, New Jersey: Princeton University Press.

Cooper, Frederic Tabor, *Rider's Bermuda*, A Guidebook for Travellers (general editor Fremont Rider). New York: The Macmillan Co., 1924.

Churchill, Winston S., *The Second World War – Volume III The Grand Alliance*. London: Cassell & Co. Ltd, 1950.

Fessenden, Helen, *Fessenden, Builder of Tomorrows*. New York, Coward McCann Inc., 1940.

Gates, Henry Louis Jr, *The Classic Slave Narratives*, New York and Scarborough, Ontario: Mentor Book-New American Library, 1987.

Gerzina, Gretchen, *Black England – Life Before Emancipation*, London: John Murray, 1995.

Gray, Bessie, *A Bermuda Garden of Song*, Boston, Mass.: Marshall, Jones & Co.,1927.

Hakluyt, Richard, *The Principal Navigations, Voyages, Traffiques & Discoveries of the English Nation*, 8 vols, London: J.M. Dent & Sons, Ltd, and New York: E.P. Dutton & Co., Everyman edn, 1926.

Harris, Dr Edward C. *Bermuda Forts*, Bermuda: Bermuda Maritime Museum Press, 1997.

Hayward, Stuart, Gomez, Vicky, and Sterrer, Wolfgang (eds), *Bermuda's Delicate Balance*, Bermuda: Bermuda National Trust,1981.

Hodgson, Eva, *Second-Class Citizens, First-Class Men*, Bermuda: Bermuda Union of Teachers, undated.

Hunter, Barbara Harries, *Beyond the Crossroads*, Bermuda: Barbara Harries Hunter, 1993.

Hyde, H. Montgomery, *The Quiet Canadian,* London: Hamish Hamilton, 1963 (1st impression 1962).

Ives, Vernon A. (ed.), *The Rich Papers, Letters from Bermuda* Toronto, Buffalo, London: published for the Bermuda National Trust by the University of Toronto Press, 1984.

James, William, *The Naval History of Great Britain from the Declaration of War by France in 1793 to the Accession of George IV,* London: Richard Bentley, 1837.

Jarvis, Michael, *Bermuda's Architectural Heritage,* St George's, Bermuda: Bermuda National Trust, 1998

Johnson, Captain Charles, *A General History of the Robberies and Murders of the Most Notorious Pirates,* London: George Routledge & Sons Ltd, 1926.

Lefroy, Major-General Sir J.H. (ed.), *Historye of the Bermudaes* (believed to be by Nathaniel Butler), London: the Hakluyt Society, 1882; republished New York: Burt Franklin, undated.

Lefroy, Major-General Sir J.H., *Memorials of the Bermudas,* Bermuda: Bermuda Historical Society and Bermuda National Trust, 3rd edn, 1981.

Lloyd, Harriett Susette, *Sketches of Bermuda,* London: Cochrane & Co., 1835.

Mudd, Patricia Marirea, *Portuguese Bermudians,* Louisville, Kentucky: Historical Research Publishers, 1991.

Musson, Nellie E., *Mind the Onion Seed,* Bermuda: Musson's, 1979.

Newman, Peter C. *Company of Adventurers,* Vol. I, Ontario: Penguin Books Canada Ltd, 1985.

Packwood, Cyril Outerbridge, *Chained on the Rock – Slavery in Bermuda,* New York: Eliseo Torres & Sons, and Bermuda: Baxters Ltd, 1975.

Packwood, Cyril Outerbridge, *Detour – Bermuda, Destination – US House of Representatives,* Bermuda: Baxters Ltd, 1977.

Philip, Ira, *Freedom Fighters – From Monk to Mazumbo,* London: Akira Press, 1987.

Raby, Ormond, *Radio's First Voice,* Toronto: Macmillan of Canada, 1970.

Roberts, Kenneth, *Henry Gross and his Dowsing Rod,* New York: Doubleday & Co., Inc., 1951.

Robinson, Dr Kenneth E., *The Berkeley Education Society's Origins and Early History.* Pembroke: Berkeleye Education Society, 1962.

Robinson, Dr Kenneth E., *Heritage,* Basingstoke: Macmillan Education, 1979.

Robinson, Dr Kenneth E., unpublished thesis on the history of education, 1952.

Rushe, George, *Your Bermuda*, Bermuda, 1995.

Smith, James E., *Slavery in Bermuda*, New York: Vantage Press, 1976.

Smith, Captain John, *The Generall Historie of Virginia, New England and the Summer Isles*, Glasgow: James Maclehose and Sons, 1907.

Smith, Sir Harry, ed. G.C. Moore Smith, *The Autobiography of Sir Harry Smith 1787–1819*. London: John Murray, 1910.

Sterrer, Wolfgang, *Bermuda's Marine Life*, Bermuda: Bermuda Natural History Museum and Bermuda Zoological Society, 1992.

Sterrer, Wolfgang, *Bermuda's Shore Plants and Seaweeds*, unpublished MS, undated.

Sterrer, Wolfgang, *How Many Species are there in Bermuda?*, unpublished MS, undated.

Sterrer, Wolfgang, with Christine Schoepfer-Sterrer, *Marine Fauna and Flora of Bermuda*, New York: John Wiley, 1986.

Stewart, Robert, *Bermuda, an Economy which Works*, Bermuda: Robert Stewart (printed by Island Press), 1997.

Tatem, Sandy, *US Naval Station, Bermuda, 1941–1968*, unpublished MS, 1970.

Tredree, H.L., *The Strange Ordeal of the Normandier*, Boston and Toronto: Little Brown & Co., 1958 (published in Britain under the title *Blackwater*).

Tucker, Nathaniel, *The Bermudian*, Hull: Joseph Simmons, 1808.

Walker, Mrs Norman (ed. Dwight Franklin Henderson), *The Private Journal of Georgiana Gholson Walker, 1852–1865*, Tuscaloosa, Alabama: Confederate Publishing Co., Inc., 1963.

Wardman, Elfrida L. *The Bermuda Jubilee Garden Book*, Bermuda: Garden Club of Bermuda, 1971.

Whittingham, Major (under the pseudonym 'A Field Officer'), *Bermuda, a Colony, a Fortress and a Prison*, London: Longmans Green, 1857.

Wilkinson, Henry C., *The Adventurers of Bermuda*, Oxford: Oxford University Press, 2nd edn, 1958.

Wilkinson, Henry C., *Bermuda from Sail to Steam*, 2 vols, Oxford: Oxford University Press, 1973.

Wilkinson, Henry C., *Bermuda in the Old Empire*, London: Geoffrey Cumberledge and Oxford University Press, 1950.

Zuill, William E.S., *Bermuda Sampler*, Bermuda: Bermuda Book Store, 1937.

Zuill, William E.S., *Bermuda Journey*, New York: Coward McCann, 1st edn, 1946

Zuill, William E.S., *Tom Moore's Bermuda Poems*, Bermuda, W.E.S. Zuill, 1984.

Zuill, William S., *The Pirate Menace*, unpublished MS, 1997.

Zuill, William S., *St Mark's Church, A History*, Smith's Parish, Bermuda: St Mark's Church Vestry, 1986.

Journals

Anderson, Ted, 'From the Steeple', church bulletin of the first Church Congregational, Windsor, Connecticut, September 1996.
Bermuda Historical Quarterly, Vols 7, No. 2 (April–June 1950), and Vol. 19, No. 2; Vol. 20, Nos 1 and 2 (Spring and Summer 1963), Hamilton.
Bermuda Journal of Archaeology and Maritime History, Vol. 1 (1989), Bermuda, Bermuda Maritime Museum Association.
Craven, Wesley Frank, *An Introduction to the History of Bermuda*. Williamsburg, *William and Mary College Quarterly*, 1937–8.

INDEX

Note: page numbers in *italics* refer to illustrations